KU-435-167

ELISABETH LAMBERT ORTIZ
THE FLAVOUR OF LATIN AMERICA
RECIPES AND STORIES

Prose and poetry selected by Nick Caistor

LATIN AMERICA BUREAU

© 1998 Elisabeth Lambert Ortiz

First published 1998

Latin America Bureau (Research and Action) Ltd
1 Amwell Street, London EC1R 1UL

The Latin America Bureau is an independent research and publishing organisation. It works to broaden public understanding of issues of human rights and social and economic justice in Latin America and the Caribbean.

Selected prose and poems compiled and translated by Nick Caistor with additional selections by Helen Collinson

Illustrations by Jane Smith

Edited by Helen Collinson and Liz Morrell

With thanks to Mike Roy, Emily Walmsley and Raquel Caravia

Designed by Andy Dark

A CIP catalogue record for this book is available from the British Library

ISBN: 1 899365 19 2

Printed by Russell Press, Nottingham NG7 3HJ

CONTENTS

Day of splendour
day of plenty
the harvest weighs
heavy on my lap.

Open doors my friends
doors and windows
invite everyone
into my home.

Give them all bread,
shelter.
Don't scare away the doves
if they fly down.

Rosario Castellanos

CORN

CORN

When Christopher Columbus arrived in the Americas, he found not only an unknown continent but a whole world of food totally new to Europeans. Here, no one ate bread. There was no wheat; instead there was a plant which the Indians of what is now the Dominican Republic called *mahis*. This has come down to us as maize, or corn. Its botanical name is *Zea mays* and it is believed to have been developed by the ancient Aztecs about 5,000 years ago from a wild Mexican grass called *teocincle*.

Maize was more than just food to the ancient peoples of America. It was the focal point of religion which was built around the Gods of corn. For the Maya, whose empire stretched from Western Honduras in Central America and into Yucatán and Chiapas in Mexico, language, ritual, and the calendar were all based on corn. The greatest of the corn gods was Quetzalcoatl. He was a descendant of the great god, Kukulkan, who is said to have founded the city of Chichen Itzá in Yucatán, the ruins of which can still be visited today. One of his emblems was sprouting maize. Even today, maize is still important to Mayan culture in Guatemala.

Over time, maize spread from its Mexican and Central American homeland across North America and into South America, arriving in the Inca Empire (now modern Peru) by 1500 BC. Here, a different type of corn from the Aztec-Maya type was cultivated, with large, starchy kernels. It was the Incas who invented popcorn!

Much of the history of maize is unknown but we do know that when the Pilgrim Fathers landed in what is now Massachusetts in the 1620s, their survival was partly dependent on local Indians who were cultivating maize of many kinds, including sweetcorn. One of the dishes to which the settlers were introduced for the first Thanksgiving was *succotash*, a Narragansett Indian word. This is a mixture of sweetcorn and lima beans and is still one of the traditional dishes in the Thanksgiving meal.

Today, there are many types of corn to choose from. Yellow and white corn make the familiar ground maize meal, while Peru has a purple corn which, when boiled, gives the water a delicious lemony, flowery taste, marvellous when making desserts. There is also black, red and blue corn. Blue corn from New Mexico, famous today for the exotic colour of its tortillas, was sacred to the Indians who first cultivated it.

AZTEC KITCHEN

North American corn dishes owe a great deal to the Aztecs. In the Aztec *Nahuatl* language, corn was called *tlaoll* and from ground, unleavened tlaoll, the Aztecs made a flat, round pancake which they called *tatonqui tlaxcalli tlacuelpacholli*. In the interests of simplicity, the Spanish renamed the pancakes *tortillas* (little cakes) which is also their word for omelettes. This causes some confusion but less than using the Aztec name.

Tortillas have the distinction of being the only bread made from cooked flour or *masa harina* in Spanish. The dry corn is first soaked with lime then boiled to soften it and remove the skins from the corn kernels, which are then drained and ground. The soft, moist dough produced is patted out into flat pancakes by hand. The Spanish simplified the process by inventing the tortilla press, consisting of two circles of wood hinged together with a handle to enable the tortilla maker to flatten a small ball of dough between the plates. Many Mexicans and Central Americans still make tortillas by hand, but it is an art I never mastered. I have, and use, an old-fashioned hand press made of cast iron and a more modern one made of aluminium. *Masa harina* or ground, cooked maize is now readily available in the supermarket, so tortillas are relatively easy to make these days. They can also be bought ready-made.

In the Aztec kitchen, there were no starters, appetizers or hors d'oeuvre as we know them, but Spanish writers of the early Conquest period, like Bernal Díaz del Castillo, an Army Captain with Hernán Cortés, and Father Bernadino de Sahagún, a Spanish priest who arrived in 1529, discovered numerous tortilla-based foods in the market that could be eaten by hand. The Spanish gave these the imaginative name of *antojitos* which means little whims or fancies.

The immense number of savoury nibbles that can be created from the simple tortilla is quite astonishing. *Tacos*, for example, are tortillas stuffed with a meat, poultry, seafood or vegetable mixture that can be mild or made fiery hot by chilli sauce, according to taste. Fresh hot tortillas are either rolled around a filling, or stuffed and secured with a toothpick and then fried in oil or lard until golden all over. Once their excess oil has been soaked up on paper towels, the tacos must be served immediately. Tacos are Mexico's universal snack food, available in a thousand and one varieties in the many *taquería* bars. They are now spreading all over the world, often mispronounced as 'tarcos' when they should be 'tackos'.

Tortillas are never wasted. Stale ones are used to make *chiliquiles*, which involves cutting tortillas into strips and frying them, then heating them through in a sauce of one's choice. This is essentially a left-over dish and is good for breakfast with eggs, a light lunch, or supper. In addition, there are many tortilla-based regional specialities in Mexico. There are *quesadillas* which are unbaked tortillas stuffed and folded over into a turnover shape, and pressed so that they stay shut in cooking before being fried in oil or lard, or toasted. The filling may be simple or elaborate and two of the most famous are *quesadillas de flor*, made with a stuffing of sautéed squash blossoms, and *quesadillas de huitlacoche*, using the corn fungus which has a marvellous flavour.

Quesadillas de flor were the first tortilla dish I learned to make when, shortly after I was married, my husband was transferred to Mexico from the UN headquarters in New York. I knew almost no Spanish but I was eager to learn about the food so I took to the famous San Juan market and somehow conveyed to one of the women market sellers my need for instruction. With a combination of sign language, and who knows what else, I secured both a recipe and the ingredients and carried them off to my mother-in-law's where I made authentic quesadillas de flor, rather to everyone's astonishment.

A lunch favourite are *tostadas*, tortillas that have been fried in oil or lard until golden brown and crisp, then spread with combinations of meats, fish and vegetables such as beans, lettuce, chillies, sauces and so on. The combinations depend on individual tastes as in all pre-Columbian Mexican cooking. There are other tortilla shapes such as *sopes* - boat shaped tortillas - and *panuchos* from Yucatán in which the top layer of the tortilla is thicker than usual, spread with mashed beans, topped with a layer of hard-cooked egg and put back in place before the tortilla is fried and garnished. The Yucatán kitchen has also produced *papatzules*, tortillas with pumpkin seed sauce. Finally there are the aristocrats of tortilla dishes, the *enchiladas* in which tortillas are dipped in sauce then fried, stuffed, rolled, put in a baking dish, masked with the sauce and heated through. Enchiladas make a great light luncheon dish. There are also a number of casseroles made with tortillas, soups and the curiously named dry soups.

TAMALES: FESTIVE FOOD

Tamales, as popular as tacos, made from the slightly different masa-type dough, are stuffed, wrapped in a dried corn husk and steamed. Here again there are a great many variations on a theme. It has been said that there are as many types of *tamal* as there are cooks! Tamales made with fresh corn cut off the cob called *uchepos* are a favourite in the Mexican state of Michoacán. It is said that the Emperor Moctezuma, before conquest, had a favourite sweet tamal, stuffed with strawberries and sweetened with honey. In the state of Oaxaca, tamales are steamed in plantain or banana leaves; in Peru, they are boiled in banana leaves, rather than steamed; in the southwest of the United States they are either big, fat affairs or tiny for serving with drinks. Brazil boasts sweetcorn and coconut tamales; Guatemala has *tamales negros* (black tamales) coloured with chocolate and eaten on holidays. In Nicaragua, tacos are often called *nacatmal* which means 'bad food'. This is a joke because the tamales are so good that one is apt to eat too much of them. The list could go on.

In Mexico, the tamal is festive food. When the family lived in Durango, my husband's grandmother, Doña Carmelita Sarabia de Tinoco was famous for her *tamaladas,* or tamal parties. Neighbours would help with the tamal preparation for three days beforehand. The party (any excuse would do: a wedding, an engagement, a birthday) would be held in the garden, which was large, with chairs and long tables set out buffet fashion, on which tamales were served, along with sauces, salads, bottles of tequila, quartered limes, soft drinks, beer and wine, fruits and sweetmeats. Maids with long plaits, dressed in long full skirts of printed cotton and embroidered blouses would carry in platters of fresh, hot

tamales from the kitchen and when they were eaten, more would arrive. Sometimes there was music too, a *mariachi* band, for example. A tamalada was always a very joyous occasion at which everyone ate and drank too much and went to bed after a very light supper.

The tamal turns up in modern guise in the Mexican ceremonies around *El Día de los Muertos* (Day of the Dead or All Souls Day) on 2 November, an amalgam of the old religion absorbed into Christianity. This is not a sad day but a special holiday when Mexicans visit their family graves in love, remembrance and respect. Huge bunches of a bright orange marigold, *zempazuchitl*, are taken to decorate the graves and at the graveside picnic, there is a special round coffee cake called *pan de muertos* (bread of the dead). This is decorated with a cross made of dough, baked in the form of alternating bones and teardrops with a knob in the centre. The dead participate symbolically in the picnic-feast. All through Mexico, in cities, towns and villages, candy skulls inscribed with the name of recipients are sold. I found it disconcerting to be given one with my name on it. Nibble on your future.

The most elaborate celebration, with strong echoes of the pre-Christian past, is on the small, Mexican island of Jantizio in Lake Pátzcuaro in Michoacán. Two days beforehand the men of the village go duckhunting, using traditional harpoons instead of guns. The women cook the meat in a chilli sauce and then stuff tamales with it. On All Souls Eve they take the tamales and bunches of marigolds and a candle for each family member who has died. With the older children, they keep a night-long vigil at the graves while the men keep vigil at home. The following day the family feasts on the tamales, with *atole* (maize gruel), coffee, *pulque* (maguey cactus beer), beer and tequila and pan de muertos for dessert. It is believed that the dead take part in the feast in a mystical way during the night of vigil.

SOUTH AMERICA

Maize dishes turn up all over South America. In the Andes, thick, doughy pancakes called *arepas* are made from maize flour, using a recipe dating back to Incan times. Still popular in Venezuela and Colombia, I have enjoyed arepas in Caracas with the doughy middle pulled out and the remaining crusty shell spread lavishly with the local cream cheese. Bolivia has a delicious chicken dish with a cooked corn topping. Brazil makes a sauce of puréed corn; in Chile there is a dish of cranberry beans, pumpkin and corn, to name a few of Latin America's regional delights.

Alongside other vegetables from the Americas, such as potatoes, yams, sweet potatoes and cassava, corn has made an important contribution to people's diets the world over. It is rightly recognized as one of the greatest gifts of the Americas to the rest of the world. In Latin America itself, corn remains an extremely popular foodstuff, not to be supplanted either by wheat or by rice which have been introduced in more recent history.

Corn Tortillas

To make tortillas you will need a tortilla press, a small plastic bag, cut open and halved to form plastic sheets for lining the press, and *masa harina*, tortilla flour, available packaged dry and ready to use.

For 16 tortillas with a diameter of 12.5cm/5"

275 g/10 oz masa harina (tortilla flour)
300 ml/11 fl oz lukewarm water
1 teaspoon salt (to taste)

In a bowl combine the masa harina, salt if using, and **225 ml/8 fluid oz** of the water and mix to a soft dough. The dough should hold together and be flexible. Test a small ball on the press. If it is too moist, it will stick to the plastic used to line the press; if it is too dry it will crumble. Add more flour or water as appropriate. Scrape off and return the test dough to the bowl. It does not hurt the dough to be handled. If necessary, gradually add the rest of the water. It is impossible to specify the exact amount of water, as fresh dough needs less water and older dough more. On a rainy day, even moisture in the air can affect its consistency. But with practice it soon becomes second nature and it is easy enough to add more flour or more water. The dough is very accommodating.

When the dough is the right consistency, line the press with the plastic sheets. Divide the dough into 16 small balls each about the size of a small egg, and press, one at a time to a thin pancake 12.5cm/5" across. Peel off the top piece of plastic and put the tortilla, plastic side up, in the palm of the left hand. Peel off the plastic and flip the tortilla onto a moderately hot ungreased *comal* or griddle set over a low heat and cook until the edges begin to curl (about 1 minute). Using your fingers or a spatula, turn the tortilla over and cook for another minute. It will be lightly flecked with brown. To make the tortilla puff up, press the top lightly with a spatula or spoon when the second side is cooking. It will collapse when taken off the griddle but makes stuffing the tortilla easier for dishes such as *panuchos*.

Stack the tortillas in a cloth napkin and repeat with the rest of the dough. When all the tortillas are stacked, fold the napkin over them and wrap in aluminium foil. Put them into a warm 70°C/150°F oven where they will stay warm for hours. Or, of course eat them as soon as they are cooked. To warm cold tortillas, pat them between damp hands and put over a low direct heat, turning constantly for about 30 seconds.

For making *tostadas*, the tortillas need to be slightly larger - 15cm/6" is a more convenient size.

Flour Tortillas

In the north of Mexico, maize does not grow very well, as it needs more water than the semi-arid land there can offer. The Spanish introduced wheat to the region, leading to the invention of wheat flour tortillas. These are particularly good with roast kid (baby goat), another northern speciality. The flourishing *cabrito* (kid) restaurants of the north serve delicious meals of roast kid, flour tortillas, *guacamole* and pickled *jalapeño* chillies.

> 225 g/ 8 oz plain flour
> 2-3 tablespoons vegetable shortening
> 1/2 teaspoon of salt
> 1 teaspoon baking powder
> 125-175 ml/ 4-6 fl oz warm water

Flour tortillas are easy to make. In a bowl sift together the flour, salt and baking powder. Rub the shortening into the flour mixture until it resembles coarse meal. Add 125 ml/4 fl oz of the warm water and mix to a fairly stiff dough that can be gathered into a ball. If necessary add more water, 1 tablespoon at a time. Knead the dough until it is smooth. Divide the dough into 12 balls and set on a flat surface. Cover with a plastic wrap and let rest for 30 minutes.

On a lightly floured surface, roll out each ball of dough to a 17 cm/7" circle. Have ready an ungreased griddle or comal heated to medium and bake for 1/2 to 1 minute, the underside will have brown patches. Flip over and bake on the other side for 1/2 to 1 minute. Wrap the tortillas immediately to stop them becoming hard and inflexible.

The gods made the first Maqya-Quices out of clay. Few survived. They were soft, lacking strength; they fell apart before they could walk.

Then the gods tried wood. The wooden dolls talked and walked but were dry; they had no blood or substance, no memory and no purpose. They didn't know how to talk to the gods, or couldn't think of anything to say to them.

Then the gods made mothers and fathers out of corn. They moulded their flesh with yellow and white corn.

The women and men of corn saw as much as the gods. Their glance ranged over the whole world. The gods breathed on them and left their eyes forever clouded, because they didn't want people see over the horizon.

POPOL VUH, The religious book of the Mayas. Quoted in Eduardo Galeano, **Memory of Fire**

Tamales

Tamales are eaten in Mexico, Venezuela, Colombia, Guatemala and Peru. They are also popular in the south west of the United States. A single one is called a tamal.

I still have a recipe given me by one of my husband's relatives. It was not for beginnners as it was for 300 tamales - just enough, I was told, for a *tamalada*.

The maize flour used to make tamales is coarser than the *masa harina* flour used for making tortillas but if tamal flour is not available, then masa harina will do fine. It is important to have good quality lard. Tamales are steamed, filled or unfilled, in dried corn husks. In Oaxaca in Southwest Mexico they are steamed in banana leaves, giving them a subtly different taste and texture. 'Blind' or unfilled tamales, made with a layer of dough about 1.2 cm/1/4" thick, are served with *Mole Poblano de Guajolote* and sometimes as a simple supper with hot chocolate or the Mexican corn drink, *atole*. Tamales with sweet fillings are eaten as a dessert while half-size ones are sometimes served as appetizers, though this is more usual in the United States than in Mexico. Popular in the Mexican states of Michoacán and Jalisco are *uchepos*, tamales made with fresh corn (instead of dry flour).

> Dried cornhusks (or sheets of greaseproof/wax paper measuring 20cm/8" × 10cm/4")
> 75g/3oz lard
> 275g/10 oz masa harina (or flour for tamales/ *'harina para tamales'*, if available)
> 1 teaspoon salt
> 1 teaspoon baking powder
> 350ml/12 fl oz lukewarm chicken stock

Soak the corn husks in hot water to soften them for about half an hour. Then shake them to get rid of the excess water and pat them dry with a kitchen towel. Cream the lard until it is very light and fluffy. In a bowl, combine the flour, salt and baking powder, mixing well. Gradually beat the flour mixture into the lard, alternating with the stock to make a slightly loose dough. Continue beating until all the ingredients are combined. To test whether the dough is ready, take a small piece and put it into the surface of the water. If it floats, the dough is ready. If it sinks, beat the dough some more. It should be very light.

Have ready the filling. Spread 1 tablespoon of the dough in the centre of each corn husk, leaving room to fold over the ends at top and bottom. Put a tablespoon of the filling in the centre of the dough and fold the dough over so that it completely covers the filling. Then fold in the top and bottom of the corn husk. Put the tamales into a steamer with the bottom ends of the cornhusks at the bottom. Cover and steam for about an hour, or until the dough comes away from the husks.

In many parts of Latin America, banana leaves are used instead of corn husks. Cut the leaves into 23cm/9" × 18 cm/7" pieces and spread about 1.5 tablespoons of the dough across the middle of the leaf in size of a rectangle about 10 cm/4" × 7.5 cm/3". Spread with the filling then fold the leaf at the bottom edge over the filling, then the leaf at the top edge and then the sides to make a parcel. Stack in a steamer and steam for 1 hour.

Sheets of greaseproof/wax paper measuring 20 cm/8" × 10 cm/4" can be used instead of corn husks or banana leaves, though some of the flavour will be lost.

Tamal fillings. Meat or poultry for filling tamales should always be boneless and shredded or cut into small pieces. *Mole Poblano* and *Picadillo* make good fillings (see Sauces), as do many of the taco fillings. Choose any filling which has meat or chicken with a sauce. For sweet tamales (*tamales de dulce*), add 125g/4oz to 225g/8 oz sugar to the basic dough, according to taste. For the filling, mix together some raisins, slivered almonds and chopped lemon peel and put a tablespoon on the dough and fold and steam in the usual way. Chopped and mixed candied fruits such as pineapple, peaches and cherries, or strawberry preserve are also good.

A fter a smooth ride of three hours and a half, at a moderate trot, we reached the foot of the hills, and stopped to breakfast, at a collection of wretched hovels, made, as I have before described, of stones loosely piled up.

We found abundance, notwithstanding this appearance of wretchedness. Excellent mutton - and in every hut I entered, there was one of the family preparing tortillas for the rest. The people were tolerably clean, and appeared healthy and contented. The interior of every hut, which is not more than eight or ten feet square, is ornamented with bad pictures of our Saviour or of the Virgin, and many had a taper burning before these household Gods. I promised some time back, to describe the method of making tortillas, and will now endeavour to do so. The Indian corn is put into a large earthen velleo of water, and a very small quantity of lime is added, less than one ounce to two gallons. It is kept for two to three hours near the fire to simmer, (is not that the technical term?) which softens it and takes off the husk. The operator is provided with a stone eighteen inches long, and a foot wide, a little concave, on which the corn is laid, and it is mashed with a stone formed like a paste roller. This is held firmly, and being passed backwards and forwards over the corn, soon crushes it to a fine paste. So prepared, it is patted into a flat circular cake extremely thin, and is cooked on the earthen pan placed on the fire.

The maidens all perform this operation with great dexterity and cleanliness. They have a jar of water by their side, into which they constantly dip their hands, to prevent the paste sticking to their fingers.

I do not like the tortillas as well as the corn bread or hoe cake of our country, but they are very palatable, and the natives live on them. They eat them with beans, and a sauce made with lard and Chile pepper, which they spread on the tortillas as thick as we do butter on bread. At this place the tortillas are blue. A great deal of the Indian corn in this country is coloured.

JOEL ROBERTS POINSETT, **Notes on Mexico Made in the Year of 1822**

Tacos

Tacos are simply tortillas wrapped around a filling. Taco fillings are an irresistible challenge to the creative cook as almost any ingredients can be added, within the framework of the Mexican kitchen. There is no real need for set recipes if the following guidelines are followed. Beef, pork or chicken are simmered in stock, cooled in the stock, lifted out, patted dry and shredded. Chorizo sausage is

skinned, crumbled and fried, eggs are scrambled, cheese is cut into strips (mild cheddar is a good substitute), boiled ham is chopped, so are chillies, lettuce and tomatoes.

> Ham filling for 12 tacos:
> 12 tortillas
> 225g/8oz ham, finely chopped
> 1 tablespoon of onion, finely chopped
> 1 clove garlic, chopped
> 225g/8oz tomatoes, peeled, seeded and chopped
> fresh or canned serrano or jalapeño chillies to taste, sliced
> 75g/3oz softened cream cheese.

Combine the ingredients and then fill the tortillas. Put a little *guacamole* (see Salads) on top of the filling before folding over the tortilla (and eating). Do not use guacamole if the taco is to be fried, in which case serve the guacamole separately. For a chorizo taco filling, add cheddar cheese, or refried beans, or both, and if liked, freshly cooked potatoes cut into small cubes and fried with the chorizo sausage. Chipotle chillies are good with this filling. Any kind of shredded meat with a sauce can be used, such as *Mole Poblano* consisting of shredded turkey in a rich sauce; in short, whatever the kitchen has to offer.

To fry tacos, stuff in the usual way, secure with a toothpick and fry in shallow oil or lard, starting with the open (toothpick secured edge) on top for about 1 minute. Take out the toothpick and fry the other side for another minute, so that the taco is lightly golden all over. Eat immediately. Tacos can be garnished with radishes, onion rings, sliced tomatoes and avocado, and shredded lettuce. In the south west of the United States the tortilla is folded into a U shape, fried crisp and stuffed generously. This kind of taco shell is also sold ready-shaped in most major supermarkets.

Tortilla sellers with their babies in shawls on their backs and a basket carried on a roundlet upon their heads, and those who had no child, with their shawl around the basket in the form of a curtain which fell on either side of their ears to shield them from the force of the sun, a gaily colored shift, petticoats and underskirts tucked up into their skirts, and very clean bare feet which scarcely touched the ground as they went running by. Goyo Yic could tell them by their quick, continuous pat-pat-pattering gait, as though they were making tortillas of earth, and because they would catch their breath with a gasp of a woman milling maize as she changes the rhythm of her hand on the grindstone.

MIGUEL ANGEL ASTURIAS, **Men of Maize**

Enchiladas Rojas
Chorizo-stuffed Tortillas with Red Chilli Sauce

The most elegant of the tortilla dishes are *enchiladas* which can be eaten for lunch or dinner. There are many different types of enchiladas but this is a particularly popular one.

Make 24 tortillas with a diameter of 10cm/4" and keep them warm.
For the filling:
6 dried ancho chillies
450g/16oz tomatoes, peeled, seeded and chopped
2 onions, finely chopped
1 large clove garlic, chopped
1/2 teaspoon dried crumbled epazote (if available) or
1 tablespoon finely chopped fresh coriander
5 tablespoons lard or vegetable oil
1/4 teaspoon sugar
salt to taste
225 ml/8 fl oz double cream
2 large eggs, lightly beaten
6 chorizo sausages, skinned and chopped
50 g/ 2 oz freshly grated parmesan cheese

Rinse the chillies in cold water, pat dry, remove the stems, veins and seeds and tear them roughly into pieces. Put them in a bowl and pour 225 ml/8 fl oz hot water over them. Soak for about 30 minutes. Transfer the chillies, the soaking water, the tomatoes, half the onion, the garlic, the *epazote* or coriander to a food processor and reduce to purée. In a heavy frying pan, heat 2 tablespoons of the lard or oil, pour in the purée and cook over a moderate heat for 5 minutes, stirring constantly. Season with the sugar and salt to taste. Remove from the heat and whisk in the cream and eggs in a stream. Set aside.

In a frying pan heat 1 tablespoon of lard or oil and sauté the chopped sausages over a moderate heat for about 5 minutes, stirrring constantly. Lift out with a slotted spoon to a bowl and stir in 75 ml/3 fl oz of the sauce and 1/3 of the grated parmesan. Now heat the remaining 3 tablespoons of lard or oil in a frying pan. Working with one tortilla at a time and using kitchen tongs, dip the tortilla quickly in the sauce, let the excess drip off, then fry in the lard or oil until it is limp and pliable, a matter of about 3 seconds. Then transfer to a work surface. This is rather messy. The alternative is to reverse the process by frying the tortilla until limp, and then dipping it in the sauce afterwards. Purists claim the first method gives a better flavour, but the difference is not a major one.

Spread each tortilla with some of the chorizo mixture and roll up, transferring each tortilla to a shallow, oiled, baking dish. When all the tortillas are in a dish, sprinkle with the remaining onion, warm the sauce and pour it over the enchiladas. Then sprinkle with the remaining parmesan and bake in a preheated 180°C/350°F oven for 20 minutes, or until heated through. *Serves 6.*

W hoever gets up first, lights the fire. She makes the fire, gets the wood hot and prepares everything to make tortillas. She heats the water. The one who gets up next washes the *nixtamal* (cauldron in which maize is cooked) outside, and the third one washes the grinding stone, gets the water ready and prepares everything needed for grinding the maize. In our house, I made the food for the dogs. My father had a lot of dogs because of the animals which came down from the mountain. These dogs guarded our animals. It was my job to make food for them. Their food was the hard core of the maize, the cob. With time, the cobs rot and go soft, and are cooked with lime. Then it's all ground up for the dogs' food. Lime makes our dogs strong, otherwise they'd all die. They don't eat our food which is maize, but, sometimes, when there's no maize, we eat the dogs' food.

RIGOBERTA MENCHÚ, **I, Rigoberta Menchú: An Indian Woman in Guatemala**

Quesadillas

Quesadillas are one of Mexico's most popular street foods, great as a starter for a light lunch or to serve with drinks. They are best described as turnovers, made from unbaked tortillas and stuffed with a variety of fillings, either toasted on a griddle or fried until golden brown on both sides in oil or lard. The dough can be varied by adding chillies or cheese etc. Two of the most popular fillings are *huitlacoche*, a mushroom-like fungus that grows on corn, and *flor de calabaza*, squash blossoms. These are not readily available even in Mexico.

To make 12 quesadillas with a diameter of 10cm/4"

For the dough:
275g/10oz masa harina (tortilla flour)
2 tablespoons plain flour
1/2 teaspoon baking powder
1/2 teaspoon salt
2 tablespoons melted lard or vegetable shortening
1 large egg, lightly beaten
125 ml/4 fl oz milk

In a bowl combine the dry ingredients, mixing thoroughly. Whisk in the egg, the melted lard or vegetable shortening and enough milk to form a fairly stiff dough. Make tortillas the usual way with the tortilla press, put some filling just off the centre of the tortilla, then fold it over to form a turnover, press the edges together to seal, set aside until all the dough is used.

Preheat a griddle to medium hot and cook the quesadillas for about 3 minutes on each side, or heat oil or lard in a frying pan to a depth of about 1.2cm/1/2" and fry the quesadillas for 2 to 3 minutes on each side. As they are done, lift out on to the paper towels to drain and serve immediately.

For a simpler quesadilla, make tortillas in the usual way with masa harina.

Quesadilla fillings. Picadillo, chorizo with potatoes, in fact just about any of the taco fillings, cheese with a little chilli and a little epazote if available, left-over mole poblano, cooked shredded chicken or pork with a chilli sauce, or a tomato sauce with a little jalapeño added.

Arepas

Andean corn has large, starchy kernels. In Colombia and Venezuela, it is used to make *arepas*. Though very different from tortillas, arepas share the distinction of being made with cooked maize flour. The arepa is rather like a flat, disc-shaped, white bread roll. It is either buttered and eaten as bread to accompany main dishes or served on its own with the doughy inside pulled out and filled with cream cheese.

(For 8-10 arepas)
275 g/ 10 oz arepa flour
1 teaspoon salt
450 ml/ 16 fl oz water

In a bowl, mix together the arepa flour and the salt, then gradually add the water, stirring to make a fairly stiff dough. Form the dough into a ball, loosely cover the bowl and let the dough rest for about 10 minutes. Form it into 8 -10 balls and press each one out into 7.5 cm/3" across and about 1.2 cm 1/2" thick. Slightly grease a heavy griddle and cook the arepas over a moderate heat for 5 minutes on each side, then bake in a 180°C/ 350°F oven for 20 - 30 minutes, turning them two or three times during the cooking. Tap them to test whether they are cooked or not. They are ready when they sound hollow. This is important as arepas are very doughy and can taste dull and heavy if not thoroughly cooked. To remove some of the heaviness, one can pull out the middle, leaving just the crusty shell to be buttered, stuffed with cream cheese softened with cream, or stuffed with whatever takes one's fancy.

The fiesta of the corn has lasted since pre-historic times. It takes place in May, at sowing time, when the black earth disappears under its jungle of corn stalks. Corn is brought out from the storehouses, and with many legendary songs the Sun is asked to favor the new crop. The dancers parade in all their finery, the sunlight glancing off the shiny ornaments on their blouses and off the gilded trimmings which adorn the velvet of their hats. From their arms float long white streamers, resembling strange white wings.

Formerly, a portion of the corn was deposited in granaries, called *piuras*. The ceremony consisted of wrapping the corn in rich cloths, covering it with flowers and garlands of branches. For three consecutive nights these granaries were watched over with songs and feasting, thus assuring that they 'were the mothers of the new corn.' After the ceremony the priests asked of these same corn bins if they were strong enough to produce sufficient corn for the new year, and if they answered no, the corn was carried to the farms, where it was burned; new bins were filled, and the entire ceremony repeated.

Today the ritual has changed. The corn is strewn over the heads of the people. One at a time, the participants receive the grain, mumbling a ritual. The orchestra play interminably; the sad little dance tune drones on, and the dancers take their places. In their hands they grasp thick balsa flails, and shortly they begin to stamp the earth. The tempo increases. The dancers pick up the time, turning, twisting, reversing all the while with the stick held aloft. The beat becomes still more violent, making the subtle yet barbaric measures. The dancers seem to be trying to get rid of the flail - sometimes they support it with both hands, sometimes with one, sometimes just with their mouths, but never letting it go entirely. The Indian parodies, ceaselessly, the corn shaken by the strong wind; yellow, blown loose from the firm base where it has sprung up. It symbolizes the futile struggle of the elements; the frosts, the floods, the droughts. It shows the triumphant and fecund power of the Sun, the unconquerable spirit of the Indian.

FELIPE COSSIO DEL POMAR, **Imperial Cusco**

SOUPS

SOUPS

Soup plays an important role in the cuisines of Latin America. In Mexico and Colombia, for example, the main meal, or *comida* would be considered a very poor thing without it. A rich array of New World vegetables have combined with Old World imports like chicken, beef, pasta, rice, cheese, cream and eggs to add richness and variety to the continent's soups.

One soup which graphically illustrates this diversity is *callaloo*, the most famous of the creole soups. Trinidad is generally regarded as its birthplace but it is also popular in Haiti (where it is known as *calalou*), and Guadeloupe, and in Jamaica. The main, and essential, ingredients are the young leaves of certain aroids, a diverse group of tropical plants with tubers. Not all aroids have edible leaves - arthuriums, calla lilies and philodendrons cannot be used. Amongst the edible aroids are dachine, eddoe, taro, elephant ear, tannia, tanniers, and yautria, all of which taste much the same. The leaves of Swiss chard make an admirable substitute. Callaloo is a hearty soup which can be turned into a full meal, as in the French islands where it is served with a side dish of rice and grilled salt cod fish.

Indigenous to the Americas, avocados have played an important part in Latin American cooking ever since they were first cultivated in Mexico around 7000 BC. The Aztecs created *guacamole* sauce (see Sauces), while in the English-speaking Caribbean islands, avocados were known as midshipman's butter and what a treat they must have been on ship's biscuits. A relative newcomer is the beautiful pale green avocado soup, which has now spread throughout South America. In Chile, avocado soup unites New and Old Worlds as it is made with béchamel sauce. Colombia's version uses potatoes.

Peanut soup turns up all over Latin America. No one version is exactly the same as another and like all ingredients in Latin America, the names given to the peanut vary too. In English-speaking countries, peanuts are called ground nuts, in Cuba and many Spanish-speaking countries the peanut is *maní* and in Mexico it is *cacahuete*. The peanut, of course, is not a nut at all but a legume. It is native to both West Africa and Brazil, which some claim is supporting evidence for the continental drift theory. The Brazilian peanut is not of the same genus as its African counterpart but nevertheless, in my opinion, it is conceivable that the wild forerunner of the peanut arose before the two continents drifted apart.

Despite its name, the Jerusalem artichoke *Helianthus tuberosus* - sometimes marketed as a sunchoke), is a knobbly root vegetable of north American origin. It is a sunflower of the daisy family, and Jerusalem is a corruption of the Italian word for sunflower, *girasol*, whose head turns round to follow the sun. They were not held in very high esteem by the Europeans who first encountered them, in fact they were considered more suitable for livestock than people. I don't think this was because of their taste which is reminiscent of globe artichokes, or their texture which is pleasantly crisp, or because cooks were lazy, not caring to peel the knobbly tubers. I am afraid it was because they were found to be wind-provoking, much as beans are. The late Jane Grigson, wise in the ways of vegetables, gave me a useful tip for peeling them, that is to boil them for 10 minutes in salted water, then run them under cold water before peeling them. When they are cooked, I puree them in a food processor and then push them through a sieve to get rid of any brown bits of skin that have survived peeling. Since they are native to the north of North America and Canada, I did not find them popular in Mexican or South American cooking, though paradoxically I found them in Peru and Chile, as far as they could get from their homeland. In Chile they are called *topinambur*.

The preferred sweet potato of Latin America has dry white flesh and a pink or white skin and is called *boniato*. My favourite boniato soup is one from Brazil where the boniato is called *batata doce* (sweet potato). Cooked with corn, chillies and onions, the finished soup is a beautiful golden-yellow colour with a hint of tartness balancing the slight sweetness of the boniato. As with many of the tubers with which Latin America is so richly endowed, they make an admirable substitute for the most popular new world tuber of them all, the potato.

Of all the foods we Europeans found in the Americas, I wonder which proved the most important contribution to our own cuisine the potato, the tomato or the whole family of the capsicums and peppers? When it comes to soups, the sweet red peppers of Mexico would be my first choice. When I was first married, my husband was transferred to his homeland, Mexico, by the United Nations to head a UN Information Centre. There I hired a Oaxacan cook, Francisca. She was a Zapoteca Indian, quite beautiful, though not young, her high cheekboned face framed by long, grey plaits. One of Francisca's most wonderful creations was *Sopa de Pimientos Morrones* (Sweet Red Pepper Soup). Apart from its beautiful red colour, it has the most enticing flavour.

One of the greatest ingredients contributed by the Americas to the world kitchen was the common bean *Phaseolus vulgaris* and its many varieties. Kidney beans were first cultivated in Mexico perhaps as long ago as 7000BC. The Spanish conquerors of Mexico found the pinto bean flourishing, a bean rich in vitamin B-1. Black haricot beans, sometimes called turtle beans, are very much enjoyed as soup in the Caribbean, Mexico, and in South America.

The pumpkin is one of the *Curbita pepo* fruits of the squash-gourd family. Though a huge pumpkin may not look like it, it is related to the small patty pan squash, crookneck squash and courgettes. The West Indian pumpkin, known under its Spanish name of *calabaza* is another relative. Pumpkins are made into soup, pie, and eaten as a hot vegetable. The flowers turn up as soup, or alternatively they are lightly fried in butter or served stuffed with other ingredients. The curbitas are a very large and old family from the Americas. They are believed to be one of the vegetables cultivated by the ancient Mexicans back in 7000BC when agriculture first began in the Valley of Mexico. Later they spread all over the Americas and the Caribbean islands. A great favourite of mine is a pumpkin soup from Puerto Rico. The best pumpkin to use is the one marketed as calabaza available in Caribbean markets, but any pumpkin will do.

The fruit of the coco palm *Cocos nucifera* can be found throughout the tropical regions. Its seed, our coconut, is well adapted to travelling on its own through water as the pod holding the seed is not only large and buoyant but also more or less waterproof. There is no doubt that it floated to the Americas on ocean currents. The seeds take root on small islands and shores in the tropics. A well looked-after palm may bear as many as two hundred fruit a year. The coconut is a very desirable immigrant as every bit of the coco palm is useful. The nut can be eaten raw or cooked, coconut water makes a refreshing drink and an alcoholic drink can be made from the sweet liquid from the flower buds as it ferments easily. It can be boiled down to various sugars and the nut is also a good source of oil. The leaves are used to make fans, the coir to make mats and the hard shell is used for fuel. Coconuts are very important to the cuisines of Latin America's tropical regions, such as coastal Colombia where I once enjoyed fish soup in coconut milk. The only time-consuming part of this recipe is extracting the thick milk from the coconut, easy if you follow the instructions. For those in a hurry, or those without a coconut, use store-packaged coconut cream which can be diluted to the desired consistency.

Curaçao, in the Dutch Antilles, certainly has one of the most unusual fish soups I have ever had. A friend there, Mrs Evert M. ('Bep') Newton cooked it for me. I would never have thought of cooking corned (salt) beef with fish to make a soup but it worked surprisingly well. I found that cooks throughout the islands were adept at using something else for things they couldn't get. In the days of sail boats, produce from elsewhere often arrived late, if at all. The ingenuity of island cooks in these circumstances seems never to have failed.

Chile, Argentina, Peru, and Ecuador have splendid versions of the Spanish soup, *chupe*. This is more a stew than a soup and is a meal in itself, frequently including potatoes, eggs and cheese amongst its varied ingredients.

Sopa de Frijoles Tiernos
Green Bean Soup
CUBA

I had this soup in Cuba but it seems as if it wanders since it has been claimed by more than one country. It is simple and refreshing.

    450g/1 lb fresh green beans
    1.5 litres/2½ pints/ chicken stock
    2 onions, finely chopped
    50 ml/2 fl oz/¼ cup olive oil
    Salt, freshly ground pepper
    Oregano, dried and crumbled

Put the beans into a large saucepan with the chicken stock, bring to a simmer, cover and cook for 10 minutes. Lift out the beans to a food processor and reduce to a purée. Return them to the saucepan. Heat the oil in a small saucepan and sauté the onions until they are soft. Add them to the beans, stir to mix and season to taste with salt and pepper, and heat through. Serve sprinkled with oregano.
Serves 6.

Sopa de Apio y Chícharros
Celery and Pea Soup
URUGUAY

    1 head celery, chopped, leaves reserved
    1.5 litres/ 2½ pints/ chicken stock
    1 bay leaf
    1 clove
    45ml/3 tablespoons corn oil
    1 onion, chopped
    1 clove garlic, chopped
    2 rashers (slices) bacon, rind removed and chopped
    1 carrot, scraped and chopped
    30g/2 tablespoons plain flour
    450g/1 lb tomatoes, peeled, seeded and chopped
    900g/2 lb young peas, if frozen, defrosted
    Salt, freshly ground pepper

Put the celery into a large saucepan with the stock, bay leaf and clove, bring to a simmer, cover and simmer for 10 minutes. Set aside. Remove the bay leaf and clove. In a frying pan heat the oil and sauté the onion, garlic, bacon and carrot until the vegetables are soft. Stir in the flour and cook for 1-2 minutes. Add the tomatoes, stir and cook for 5 minutes. Add to the stock with the celery, cover and simmer for 5 minutes. Remove the solids to a food processor and reduce to a purée then push through a sieve set over the saucepan.

Season to taste with salt and pepper. Add the peas and simmer until the peas are tender, about 10 minutes. Serve garnished with the reserved celery leaves. *Serves 6.*

Sopa de Calabaza
Pumpkin Soup
PUERTO RICO

30ml/2 tablespoons corn oil
1 onion, finely chopped
2 cloves garlic, chopped
30g/2 tablespoons fresh coriander leaves, chopped
675g/1 1/2 lb West Indian pumpkin, peeled and chopped
1.5 litres/2 1/2 pints chicken stock
For the garnish: 1/2 sweet red pepper, peeled and chopped
1/2 sweet green pepper, peeled and chopped
Salt and freshly ground pepper

Heat the oil in a frying pan and sauté the onion, garlic and coriander until the onion is soft. Set aside. In a saucepan combine the pumpkin and the chicken stock and simmer until the pumpkin is tender. Add the onion mixture and simmer 5 minutes longer to blend the flavours. Season to taste with salt and pepper. In the oil remaining in the frying pan, adding a little more if necessary, sauté the peppers for 3-4 minutes. Drain on paper towels and add to the soup. *Serves 6.*

Sopa de Frijol Negro
Black Bean Soup
VENEZUELA

450g/1 lb black haricot beans
1 medium onion, chopped
2 cloves garlic, chopped
2.5ml/1/2 teaspoon ground cumin
5ml/1 teaspoon hot red chilli, dried and crumbled
1.5 litres/2 1/2 pints beef stock
Salt

Rinse and pick over the beans and put them to soak overnight. When ready to cook drain and rinse the beans and discard the soaking water. Put them into a large saucepan with the stock and the onion, garlic, cumin and chilli and bring to a simmer. Cover and cook the beans over low heat until they are very soft, about 2 1/2 hours. The time will vary according to the age of the beans. Purée the beans in a food processor using some of the liquid to help and doing this in batches if necessary. Return the purée to the saucepan, season with salt and heat through. Serve garnished with a little chopped hard-boiled egg if liked. *Serves 6.*

Sopa de Calabacita
Courgette Soup
MEXICO

450g/1 lb courgettes, coarsely chopped
1 onion, chopped
1 fresh jalapeño chilli, seeded and chopped
1.5 litres/2¹/2 pints chicken stock
1 large egg yolk
120ml/4 fl oz double cream

In a large saucepan combine the courgettes, onion, jalapeño and chicken stock and simmer, covered, until the vegetables are tender, about 15 minutes. Transfer the solids to a food processor and reduce to a purée. return the purée to the stock, stir to mix and season to taste with salt. Set aside.

In a bowl beat the egg yolk together with the cream and stir in about 250ml/8 fl oz of hot soup, then whisk the mixture into the saucepan. Heat the soup through, stirring, but do not let it boil. Serve with fresh hot tortillas. *Serves 6.*

Sopa de Pescado con Coco
Fish Soup with Coconut Milk
COLOMBIA

50g/2 oz butter
1 onion, finely chopped
1-2 small fresh hot red or green chillies, seeded and chopped
30g/2 tablespoons plain flour
Coconut cream
1.2 litres/2 pints fish stock
450g/1 lb any non-oily firm-fleshed white fish cut into 5cm/2 inch pieces
Salt

In a saucepan heat the butter and onion and the chillies and sauté until the vegetables are soft. Stir in the flour and cook, stirring for a minute or two. Set aside. Mix the coconut cream with the fish stock to the consistency of very light cream. Stir into the saucepan and cook over low heat for 5 minutes. Add the fish, season to taste with salt and cook for 5 minutes longer. *Serves 6.*

Sopa de Topinambur
Jerusalem Artichoke Soup
PERU

30ml/2 tablespoons butter or corn oil
1 onion, finely chopped
1 clove garlic, chopped
675g/1¹/2 lb Jerusalem artichokes, scraped and coarsely chopped

1.5 litres/2¹/2 pints chicken stock
Salt, freshly ground pepper

In a saucepan heat the butter or oil and sauté the onion and garlic until the onion is soft. Add the artichokes and cook for 3-4 minutes. Pour in the chicken stock and simmer until the artichokes are soft, about 20 minutes. Season to taste with salt and pepper. Remove the solids from the soup and purée them in a food processor then push them through a sieve to remove any remaining brown skin. Return the purée to the liquid, stir to mix and heat through.

If liked, garnish the soup with chopped fresh coriander or flat-leafed parsley leaves. *Serves 6.*

Sopa Crema de Elotes
Cream of Corn Soup
PARAGUAY

Corn soups abound in Latin America. I had this one in Paraguay.

50g/2 oz butter
1 onion, finely chopped
225g/8 oz tomatoes, peeled, seeded and chopped
450g/1 lb frozen corn kernels, defrosted
1.2 litres/2 pints chicken stock
250ml/8 fl oz double cream

In a large saucepan heat the butter and sauté the onion until it is soft. Add the tomato and cook, stirring until the mixture is well-blended. Add the corn kernels and the stock, bring to a simmer and cook, covered, for 5 minutes. Transfer the solids to a food processor and process to a purée. Put through a sieve set over the saucepan, pressing hard to extract all the flavour. Season with salt and stir in the cream. Stir to mix and heat through. *Serves 6.*

Sopa de Maní
Peanut Soup
ECUADOR

30ml/2 tablespoons peanut or corn oil
1 onion, finely chopped
2 cloves garlic, chopped
1 sweet red pepper, seeded and chopped
1 guajillo or any very hot dried chilli as the Bolivian ají (chilli) is not available
225/8 oz tomatoes, peeled and chopped
115g/4 oz toasted peanuts, finely ground
1.5 litres/2¹/2 pints chicken stock
30g/2 tablespoons fresh coriander leaves, chopped

Heat the oil in a frying pan and sauté the onion, garlic, and sweet pepper until they are soft. Set aside. Toast the chilli in an ungreased frying pan, pull off the stem and shake out the seeds. Tear into pieces and soak for 20 minutes in warm water barely to cover, turning from time to time. Drain and put into a food processor with the tomatoes and the solids from the frying pan.

Process to a puree and return to the frying pan with the peanuts. Cook, stirring, over low heat for 5 minutes then transfer to a saucepan with the stock and cook over low heat, covered, for 15 minutes to blend the flavours. Serve garnished with the coriander. Smooth peanut butter may be used instead of the finely ground peanuts. *Serves 6.*

Chupe
Potato Soup
ARGENTINA

> 50ml/2 fl oz corn oil
> 2 onions, finely chopped
> 1 sweet red pepper, seeded and chopped
> 450g/1 lb potatoes, peeled and cut into 1cm/1/2 inch cubes
> 30g/2 tablespoons flat-leafed parsley, chopped
> 1.5 litres/21/2 pints beef stock
> Salt, freshly ground pepper

Heat the oil in a saucepan and add the onion. Sauté until it is lightly golden. Add the sweet red pepper and the potatoes, stir to mix and cook for 2-3 minutes. Add the parsley, pour in the stock and simmer for 30 minutes. Season to taste with salt and pepper. *Serves 4-6.*

Sopa de Batata Doce y Elotes
Sweet Potato and Corn Soup
BRAZIL

Variations of this soup are popular all over Latin America. The sweet potato used is the boniato with white flesh. It is hardly sweet. The orange Louisiana yam, which is not a yam, but a sweet potato should not be used as it is too sweet.

> 1 onion, finely chopped
> 50ml/2 fl oz corn oil
> 450g/1 lb sweet potatoes, peeled and chopped
> 1.5 litres/21/2 pints chicken stock
> 225g/8 oz frozen corn kernels, defrosted
> 1-2 serrano chillies, seeded and chopped
> Salt
> To garnish: Chopped fresh coriander leaves or flat-leafed parsley

In a saucepan sauté the onion in the corn oil until it is soft. Add the sweet potatoes and sauté for 2-3 minutes longer. Pour in the chicken stock and simmer, covered until the potato is tender, about 20 minutes. Transfer the solids to a food processor and reduce to a purée. Return the purée to the saucepan with the stock and add the corn kernels and serranos. Simmer 5 minutes, season with salt and serve, garnish, if liked, with coriander or parsley. *Serves 6.*

Sopa de Tomates
Tomato Soup
CHILE

1.5kg/3 lb tomatoes, peeled and chopped
50ml/2 fl oz olive oil
1 onion, finely chopped
2 cloves garlic, chopped
10g/2 teaspoons sweet paprika
Salt, 5g/1 teaspoon sugar
1.5 litres/2½ pints chicken stock

Heat the oil in a large saucepan and add the onion and garlic. Sauté until the onion is tender then add the tomatoes and paprika, cook for 5 minutes longer. Purée the solids in a food processor then rub through a sieve set over the saucepan. Pour in the stock, season with salt and sugar and simmer for 5 minutes. Garnish, if liked, with coriander or parsley. *Serves 6.*

Sopa de Palta or Sopa de Aguacate
Avocado Soup

2 large, ripe avocados
1 litre/1¾ pts rich chicken stock
125 ml/4 fl oz double cream
Salt, freshly white pepper
1 tablespoon fresh coriander leaves, finely chopped (optional)
Tortilla chips

Halve the avocados and remove the pits. With a fork mash the avocados, scoop out and put through a sieve into a warmed soup tureen. In a saucepan heat the stock and cream. Pour the hot mixture on to the avocados, whisking to mix. Season with the salt and pepper. Sprinkle with the coriander if using and serve immediately with tortilla chips.

If serving the soup chilled, skim the chicken stock of all fat, mix with the cream, mashed avocados, salt and pepper in a blender or food processor and blend until smooth. Pour into a tureen, cover with cling film to exclude air as this minimizes darkening. If the top of the soup darkens, stir it in as the slight darkening does not affect flavour, sprinkle with coriander and serve in chilled soup bowls. *Serves 6.*

P olitics was always one of the important condiments in the stews the Sauri family served. Josefa had known for many years that it was her ally, and to be sure it would always come to her aid, it had occurred to her once to represent it at a table alongside the salt and pepper, in the shape of a pot full of small pebbles which would rattle when shaken. With this talisman in front of her, Josefa felt confident of success whenever she was worried about a dinner party. At first, the pot filled with stones had caused her family endless mirth, but as the years went by it became a habit for them all, so they gradually forgot about it. Yet the pot was still there in the tray at the centre of the table where the different dressings, the chile, the salts and the spices were laid out.

That evening all the guests seemed to have purposely decided to put off any talk about politics. Over the consommé, the talk was of travel. Zavalza thought it was high time Emilia got to know Europe, and Diego agreed with him that one was not only different but better for having walked the streets of Paris until one knew it as well as Puebla. Josefa was extremely discreet, and did not point out that she was without ever in her life having crossed the Atlantic; with her eyes, she begged her sister across the table not to mention it. So they moved on to the chicken without disturbing the peace of their banal table talk. Perhaps everything would have continued in a similar excellent vein had it not been that Zavalza was so keen to put pepper on his meal that he confused it with the pot of pebbles, which he shook vigorously over his chicken, releasing only a torrent of sound. Everybody laughed, and spent some time poking fun at Josefa's belief in her talisman's ability to summon up politics. A few seconds later, they suddenly heard drifting up from the street the sound of a flute, which vibrated in Emilia's ears before anyone else's, and caused her to leap up from the table without a word, but with a smile on her lips as proud as if it were a sceptre in her hand.

ANGELES MASTRETTA, **Mal de Amores**

Sopa de Pimientos Morrones
Sweet Red Pepper Soup
MEXICO

     2 tablespoons peanut or corn oil
     1 medium onion, finely chopped
     2 cloves garlic, chopped
     3 large sweet red peppers, peeled (see below)
     850 ml/1 1/2 pints chicken stock
     275 ml/1/2 pint tomato juice
     Salt, freshly ground pepper

In a small frying pan heat the oil and sauté the onion and garlic until they are tender. Set aside. Peel the peppers according to the instructions (below). Remove the seeds and chop coarsely. Combine the peppers, onion and garlic in a food processor with a little of the stock and reduce to a smooth purée. Pour the mixture into a saucepan with the rest of the stock and the tomato juice. Season to taste with salt and pepper, simmer, covered, over low heat for 10 minutes. If preferred the soup can be served chilled. Garnish with a little chopped coriander. *Serves 6.*

To Peel Peppers
Choose peppers with smooth, unwrinkled skins. Stick a kitchen fork into the stem end of the pepper and toast it over a gas flame or electric burner, turning frequently until the skin burns and blisters all over. Repeat until the peppers are used up. As each one is toasted transfer it to a plastic bag, adding the peppers as they are done, Leave in the closed bag for 30 minutes. Rinse the charred part of the thin papery skin off under cold running water. Pull away any skin that does not rinse off. Toasting the peppers brings out the flavour.

Callaloo
TRINIDAD

> 450 g/1 pound callaloo leaves or spinach, Chinese spinach, or Swiss chard (sugar beet)
> 1.5 litres/2¹/₂ pts chicken stock
> 1 onion, finely chopped
> 1 large clove garlic, chopped
> 3 spring onions, trimmed and chopped using both white and green parts
> Sprig thyme or ¹/₄ teaspoon dried
> 100 g/4 oz lean salt pork cut into 1.2 cm/¹/₂-inch cubes
> 225 g/¹/₂ lb fresh, frozen or tinned crab meat
> 125 ml/4 fl oz coconut milk
> 225 g/8 oz young okras, or 275 g/10 oz package frozen okra, sliced
> Salt, freshly ground pepper
> Pickapeppa-Hot-Pepper Sauce, Tabasco or other hot sauce, to taste

Wash the greens, shake dry and chop coarsely. In a large heavy casserole or saucepan combine the greens, chicken stock, onion, garlic, spring onions, thyme and salt pork. Cover and simmer over low heat until the pork is tender. Add the crab meat, coconut milk, and okras and cook for 10 minutes longer or until the okras are tender. Season to taste with salt, pepper and hot pepper sauce.

Traditionally this would be served with Foo-foo. *Serves 6.*

Foo-foo
Pounded Green Plantain Balls
TRINIDAD AND BARBADOS

3 green (unripe) plantains, unpeeled
Salt

Choose a saucepan large enough to hold the plantains comfortably in a single layer. Put the unpeeled plantains into the saucepan and pour in enough water to cover. Do not add salt. Bring to a simmer and cook until the fruit is tender, about 30 minutes. Lift out the plantains, peel and chop coarsely and pound in a mortar until smooth. Moisten the pestle with cold water from time to time as the plantains are very sticky. Season with salt. With wet hands form the mashed fruit into small balls. Keep warm and serve with Callaloo or any créole soup. *Serves 6.*

FISH

FISH

Mexico, Central and South America are lapped by the Atlantic, Pacific, and Caribbean, resulting in a rich variety of fish.

The cold Humboldt current flowing from the Pacific tip of Chile up the coast past Peru has a profound influence on the continent's seafood. In southern Chile, the Humboldt is responsible for a rich harvest of plankton and wonderful *locos* (abalones) and *erizos* (sea urchins). The latter are so generous in size that one alone is almost enough for a light lunch. Abalone has to be tenderized and in Chile I was told of some unorthodox ways of doing this. Once removed from the shell, it is wrapped in a cloth and beaten against the ground, the floor, or any hard surface. My favourite method came from a woman who put her shucked shellfish into the washing machine and let the machine beat them into tender submission. Properly tenderized, I have enjoyed them served cold, with mayonnaise or parsley sauce.

Chile also boasts a very fine fish called *congrio*, the Spanish for conger eel or sea eel. To me, it did not taste like eel to which I am very partial, so I went to the fish market in Santiago to see what it looked like. There were all three kinds: *colorado, negro, dorado* - red, black and gold. Large fish with big heads and tapering bodies, they did look a little eel-like, but eels they were not. With the help of friends who found experts for me, I was able to track them down. They are *Genypterus chilensis* living in waters off the length of Chile's Pacific coast and up as far north as Peru. Their only relative is a fish in New Zealand waters called ling, unrelated to the European ling. When cooked, the firm flesh breaks into large flakes rather as a cod does and they can be cooked in the same way as cod or any firm fleshed, non-oily fish.

In a Peruvian beach resort just south of Lima we once had raw scallops with a squeeze of lemon juice as the only seasoning. Their shells were so magnificent that I begged the restaurant for them and still use them today. Scallops have long since disappeared from Lima's coastline. But in Lima we have also enjoyed the local *seviche*, very different from the ones I was familiar with in Mexico. Seviche, or less usually cebiche, is a very ancient dish that is believed to have originated in Polynesia. The Peruvian seviches tend to be the heartiest, the Ecuadorean ones the most original, and the Guatemalan seviche made with fresh oysters the most luxurious.

To make seviche, the seafood is immersed in lime or lemon juice and 'cooked' by the acid in the juices, sometimes with Seville orange juice as well. No other preparation is needed, but the seafood must be left to marinate for sufficient time. In Peru it is served with sweet potatoes and corn and a garnish including lettuce, onion rings, and strips of chilli. In Ecuador, where seviche is claimed to be an excellent pick-me-up after a night out, prawns and a local black conch are popular, as well as striped bass; fresh, chopped tomato and Seville orange juice are also often added. There are all manner of small variations. Mexico, for example, uses a seviche of shrimps to fill avocado halves and modifies the oily nature of *sierra*, Spanish mackerel, with citrus juices.

There is sometimes confusion over a totally unrelated dish, *escabeche*, prepared throughout the region. Escabeche is the Spanish for pickled and is a term usually used to describe a cooking method in which the food is first fried, usually in oil, then pickled or soused in oil, vinegar and seasonings. In the Spanish-speaking islands of the Caribbean, *Pescado en Escabeche* (Fish in Oil and Vinegar) is served as a first course, but in Jamaica, once a Spanish island and later British, the name has become transformed into *escovitch* or *caveached* fish, meaning pickled or soused in English. It is served both as a first course and in heartier helpings as a main course. Other foods are also pickled by the same method, poultry or game, for example. They are served hot or cold.

Colombia has a two-ocean frontage, the Pacific and the Caribbean, which accounts for its wide range of seafood. Great mountain ranges rise from the coast to a high plateau, producing a range of foodstuffs from tropical to temperate. Coconut, principally in the form of coconut milk, plays a large role. A dish that impressed me was *Rábalo Guisado en Leche de Coco* (Bass in Coconut Milk). In Colombia and Venezuela we have had many fine and hearty dishes made with striped bass and red snapper from the 'grouper' family of fish. To complicate matters, some fish is marketed as red snapper when it is not a grouper but a rockfish. So long as it is a fine, firm-fleshed, non-oily white fish, its name hardly matters for culinary purposes.

Despite the abundance of groupers in Caribbean waters, the islands have maintained their love of salt cod fish. Jamaica's national dish is Salt Fish and Ackee. Ackee is the fruit of a West African tree, *Blighia sapida*, named in honour of Captain Bligh who introduced it to the island. The tree is a handsome evergreen, the fruits scarlet. The contents inside the shell look a little like scrambled eggs: this is the aril, the edible part. The shiny black seeds are discarded. Outside Jamaica it is mostly only available tinned. The taste is delicate and complements the strongly flavoured salt cod. In Dominica the salted fish is cooked with eggs for *Salt Fish en Chemise*, while in Martinique and Guadeloupe it is combined with avocado and cassava meal to make *Féroce d'Avocat*, a 'fierceness' of avocado, which refers to the hot chillies the dish contains.

I have always been fascinated by Paraguay, a landlocked country where the local Indian language, Guaraní is spoken as much as, if not more than, Spanish. I did not feel landlocked because the eastern and most densely populated part of the country, lies between the Paraguay and Paraná rivers. The country's chief port is at Asunción, where my husband and I once stayed. It was almost like being at the seaside. I remember a Paraguayan stew I ate for lunch one day, made with a fish called *dorado* which had been caught in the great silver waterway beneath us. I found it very like Spanish dolphin, a fish not to be confused with the mammalian dolphin. It has firm white flesh and has a similar taste to a Chilean congrio.

Brazil, with its great bulge out into the Atlantic, has a great abundance of shrimps, prawns and other seafood. It also has some memorable dishes in the seafood category. There is *vatapá* (see Sauces), a dish from Bahia where food is cooked in the sauce itself, and the *moquecas*, also from Bahia. These stews, for lack of a better word to describe their complexity, come from a combination of the cooking of the indigenous Indians, Africans and Portuguese that make up the population of the region. Many originate from the *pokekas*, Indian dishes wrapped in banana leaves and cooked in a saucepan on top of the stove. The *Moqueca de Camarão*, Bahian Stew, is Brazilian cooking at its exotic best, combining African dendê (palm) oil, carrots and olive oil from the Old World with peppers and tomatoes from the New.

There I saw rivers of milk,
and fences of roast meat.
There were lakes of pure honey,
and others filled with cream,
reservoirs of port wine
and mountains of stewing steak.

The stones in São Sarué
are made of cheese or sugar.
There are wells full of coffee,
already prepared, and nice and hot,
and everything else you need
is there in great abundance

The hens lay all day,
but instead of eggs they produce roast chickens,
and the fields of wheat
produce full loaves of bread.
Butter simply rains from the sky
forming heaps there on the ground.

The fish there are completely tame,
used to the company of people.
They leave the sea and go to people's houses,
huge and fat and meaty.
The people just have to pick them up and eat them,
for they arrive all ready cooked.

MANOEL CAMILO DOS SANTOS, **Journey to São Sarué** in **Brazilian Popular Prints**

Chupe de Congrio
Fish Stew
CHILE

    1kg/2¼ lbs cod fillets, cut into 6 pieces, as a substitute for congrio
    60ml/4 tablespoons butter or oil
    2 onions, finely chopped
    2 slices white bread, soaked and squeezed out
    2.5g/½ teaspoon hot paprika
    Salt, freshly ground pepper
    2.5g/½ teaspoon oregano, crumbled
    6 cooked potatoes
    250ml/8fl oz milk
    3 hard-boiled eggs, sliced

Heat the butter or oil in a casserole, add the onions and sauté them until they are golden. Add the bread, hot paprika, salt, pepper and oregano and cook, stirring to mix, for a few minutes. Pour in the milk, stir to mix, cover the casserole and cook over low heat until the mixture forms a thick sauce. Arrange the fish fillets on the sauce, cover and cook until the fish is done. Check to see that the mixture is not drying out and add a little more milk if necessary. Serve surrounded by the potatoes and eggs. *Serves 6.*

Seviche de Corvina
Striped Bass 'Cooked' in Lime Juice
PERU

    700 g/1½ lbs fillets of striped bass or similar fish cut into 2.5cm/1-inch pieces
    2 small fresh chillies, preferably red, seeded and thinly sliced
    1 teaspoon sweet paprika
    1 large onion, thinly sliced

225 ml/8 fl oz lime juice or lemon juice
225 ml/ 8 fl oz Seville (bitter) orange juice or if not available a mix of lemon and orange juice
450g/1 lb sweet potatoes, preferably boniato, (the white type)
2 ears corn, each cut into 4 slices
Lettuce leaves

Arrange the fish in a glass or china bowl and season with salt. Add 1 of the chillies, the sweet paprika and the onion, reserving some for the garnish. Mix in the lime juice and Seville orange juice, cover and refrigerate for 3 hours, stirring once or twice, or until the fish is opaque, 'cooked' by the fruit juices.

Peel the sweet potatoes and cut into 8 slices. Drop into salted water and simmer until tender, about 20 minutes. Drop the corn slices into boiling salted water and cook for 5 minutes. Drain the sweet potatoes and corn and reserve.

Line a serving platter with lettuce leaves. Arrange the fish on the platter, garnish with the reserved onion rings and sliced chilli. Arrange the corn and sweet potato slices round the edge of the platter. Serve with *cancha*, toasted corn, if available. *Serves 6.*

A nd when the Inca wishes to eat fresh fish from the sea, and even though it was seventy or eighty leagues from the coast to Cuzco they were brought alive and twitching, which seems incredible over such a long distance over such rough and craggy roads, and they ran on foot and not on horseback, because they never had horses until the Spaniards came to this country.

M. DE MURUA, **Historia General del Perú, origen y descendencia de los Incas**

Salt Fish and Ackee

JAMAICA

450 g/1 lb salt cod fish
24 fresh ackees or 625 g/1 1/4lb tin, drained
125 g/4 oz salt pork, diced
1 large onion, finely chopped
1 or 2 small fresh hot chillies, or to taste
3 large spring onions, chopped, using white and green parts
Sprig fresh thyme, or 1/4 teaspoon dried
450 g/1 lb tomatoes, peeled and chopped
for the garnish:
6 slices bacon, fried crisp and crumbled
1 tomato, cut into 8 wedges
Parsley or watercress sprigs

Put the salt cod on to soak in cold water to cover overnight or for at least 2 hours according to the hardness and saltiness of the fish and put it on to cook in fresh water to cover. Simmer, covered, for 15-20 minutes, until the fish is tender. Drain, remove any skin and bones and flake the flesh. Set aside. If using fresh ackees, add to the fish after it has been simmering for 5 minutes. If using tinned ackees, add to the fish when it is set aside.

In a small heavy frying pan fry the salt pork until it has given up all its fat and the dice are crisp and brown. Drain and set the dice aside with the salt fish.

In the fat remaining in the pan sauté the onion until it is tender and lightly browned. Add the chillies, spring onions, thyme and tomatoes and sauté until the mixture is well blended, about 5 minutes. Add the flaked cod, ackees and salt pork dice and heat through.

Transfer the mixture to a warmed platter and garnish with the bacon, tomato wedges and the parsley or watercress sprigs. *Serves 4.*

Féroce d'Avocat
Avocado-Salt Codfish Appetizer

MARTINIQUE AND GUADELOUPE

175 g/6 oz salt codfish
1 large ripe avocado, peeled, stone removed, and chopped
175 ml/6 fl oz peanut or corn oil
50 ml/2 fl oz lime or lemon juice
1 small onion, finely chopped
1 clove garlic, crushed
2 small chillies, red or green, seeded and chopped, or to taste
2 tablespoons parsley, preferably flat continental type, finely chopped
Salt
100g/4 oz cassava meal (gari)
150 ml/5 fl oz coconut milk, or milk

Prepare the codfish in the usual way (see previous recipe) and shred it very finely. Place in a bowl with the avocado. Lightly beat together the oil and lime or lemon juice and stir in the fish and vegetable mixture. Add the onion, garlic, chillies and parsley. Add salt only if needed as the fish may still be quite salty.

In a bowl mix together the cassava meal and coconut milk just to moisten. Add to the cod avocado mix and mash all to a smooth, heavy paste adding more of the coconut milk if needed. Serve as an appetizer or spread on canapés to serve with drinks.

Corvina a la Criolla
Creole-style Bass
PARAGUAY

Though I first had this in Paraguay, the cooking method is common to many countries, and we also had it in Argentina and Chile. If liked, a little hot paprika may be added to the seasonings.

    6 175g/6oz fillets of bass or any non-oily firm-fleshed white fish
    Salt, freshly ground pepper
    50ml/2 fl oz olive oil
    2 onions, thinly sliced
    3 medium-sized potatoes, peeled and thinly sliced
    2 large tomatoes each weighing 225g/8 oz, peeled and sliced
    2 bay leaves
    250ml/8 fl oz fish stock

Season the fish with salt and pepper. Pour the oil into a flameproof casserole, preferably earthenware and arrange the fish in it. Top the fish with the onions, potatoes, tomatoes and the bay leaves, broken in halves. Pour in the fish stock, cover and set over moderate heat. Cook until the potatoes are tender adding more fish stock if necessary. Remove and discard the bay leaves and serve hot. *Serves 6.*

Merluza a la Vinagreta
Hake in Vinaigrette Sauce
ARGENTINA

This is the Argentinian version of Escabeche, popular in the entire region.

    900 g/2 lbs hake fillets or other firm-fleshed white fish, cut into 6 pieces
    Salt, preferably coarse
    Plain flour
    3 tablespoons olive oil
    2 cloves garlic, finely chopped
    3 gherkins, finely chopped
    2 hard-boiled eggs, chopped
    2 tablespoons capers
    2 tablespoons parsley, preferably flat type, finely chopped

Salt, freshly ground pepper
175 ml/6 fl oz red or white wine vinegar
175 ml/6 fl oz olive oil
For garnish: lettuce leaves

Rinse the fish and pat it dry with paper towels. Sprinkle with salt and stand in cool place for 1 hour. Rinse and dry. Dredge with flour, shaking to remove the excess. Heat the 3 tablespoons olive oil in a frying pan and sauté 10 minutes to the 2.5 cm/1 inch thickness, 5 minutes on each side. Lift the fish out into a shallow dish and pour over a sauce made by mixing the garlic, gherkins, eggs, capers, parsley, salt, freshly ground pepper and the vinegar and olive oil lightly beaten. Let the fish stand for at least 1 hour before serving. Garnish with lettuce leaves and serve as a first course. *Serves 6.*

There are many species of fish in this world. There is the fish which eats mud, the fish which chews cockroaches, the fish which is always drinking soup, making slurping noises as it does so, the fish which when it sees the pregnant female laying eggs cannot contain itself and with a flap of its tail fills the water with its sperm, turning it a milky colour all round. There is the fish which pursues shiny metals, mackerel which leap out of the water just like mullet, some almost atomic members of the croaker family, such as the toadfish, found all along the coast of Bahia, which not only smokes cigarettes but prefers them full of tar and without a filter, though these are hard to get nowadays, this fish being poisonous and stinging worse than a ray anyone foolish enough to meddle with its privates, causing them a fever and the shakes, and quite often diarrhoea, although it is a cold fish in many other areas of life. Then there are the sharks, which have to be constantly swimming, in order to avoid drowning.

It's odd I understand so much about our fish, but never manage to catch any.

JOÃO UBALDO RIBEIRO, **The Saint Who Did Not Believe in God**

Arroz con Camarones
Shrimp and Rice
DOMINICAN REPUBLIC

I have to thank my husband for this recipe. In the Dominican Republic, on a day off at the beach, he saw some locals making it for lunch, the pan over a fire of sticks. They invited him to join them, and as well as a delicious lunch he got the recipe for me. I have translated it from beach to kitchen stove.

3 tablespoons achiote oil (see page 84) or olive oil
2 medium onions, finely chopped
2 cloves garlic, chopped
450 g/1 lb long grain rice

1 litre/1³/4 pts chicken stock
250g/8 oz tomatoes, peeled, seeded and chopped
2 tablespoons fresh coriander chopped
1 bay leaf
Salt, freshly ground pepper
450g/1 lb prawns, raw if possible, chopped into 1.2 cm/¹/2 inch pieces
Oil or butter for prawns

In a large frying pan that has a lid, heat the achiote or olive oil and sauté the onion and garlic over moderate heat until the onion is tender but not browned. Stir in the rice and cook it, stirring, until it has absorbed all the oil. Do not let it brown. Add the chicken stock, tomatoes, coriander, bay leaf and salt and pepper to taste. Cover and cook over very low heat until the rice is tender and all the liquid absorbed.

If using raw prawns, heat a little oil or butter in a frying pan and toss the prawns over a fairly high heat until they are pink, about 2 to 3 minutes. Mix them gently into the rice and cook, covered for a minute or two longer. If using cooked prawns simply fold them into the rice and heat through. *Serves 6.*

Quitute Bahiano
Fish in Peanut and Coconut Sauce
BRAZIL

30g/2 tablespoons corn or peanut oil
900g/2 lb any non-oily, firm-fleshed white fish, cut into 5cm/2 inch pieces
350g/12 oz peeled prawns, preferably raw
50g/2 oz peeled and toasted peanuts
30ml/2 tablespoons plain flour
250ml/8 fl oz milk
Milk as needed
50g/2 oz coconut cream
Salt, freshly ground pepper
30ml/2 tablespoons dendê oil

In a large frying pan heat the oil and sauté the fish pieces briefly on both sides. Lift out and set aside. In a food processor combine the prawns and peanuts and reduce to a paste. In a bowl stir the milk into the flour until it is smooth. Mix in the prawn and peanut mixture. Mix the coconut cream with a little milk and stir it into the main mixture. It should be very smooth. Season with salt and pepper and pour into a saucepan. Cook, stirring, over very low heat until the sauce is the consistency of a medium béchamel. Add more milk if necessary. Lightly grease a flameproof casserole and arrange the fish and any liquid that may have collected, in it. Pour on the sauce, and cook on top of the stove, covered over low heat until the fish is cooked, about 8 to 10 minutes. Remove from the heat, uncover and gently fold in the dendâ oil. Serve with rice. 15ml/1 tablespoon rice flour may be substituted for half the plain flour, if liked. *Serves 6.*

After a full-blooded Argentinian diet of of red meat, innards and organs, Chilean fare was more often taken from the sea. But some of the seafood here made the stuff we had been gorging on seem like fairy cakes.

One stall was a solid black mountain. A man behind it, slushing around in rubber boots, was taking foot-wide pieces of this black stuff and sawing through them. Black, gnarled lumps, hairy looking without having any hair, accretions of hard core from the abyss, they should have been on a building site, not a food market. When the top of the lump was sawed off the man stuck two fingers into half a dozen holes and, with a slurp, gouged out the sloppy orange shellfish that had been living there. He flung them a long way into a bucket on the floor…

The greatest nightmare was still to come. When I looked round at the next stall I suddenly knew the meaning of fear. It looked like another mountain of accretions, a pile of aggregate, grey and crusty rather than black, a bunch of rocks with holes, little caves in them. I moved closer and flinched… A grey-pink pearly diaphragm was throbbing and a vicious curved beak clawed out from the centre. It opened and uselessly jabbed at the air. A nasty sliver of tongue darted out. I jumped back, my jaw on my chest. I pointed at the nightmare and looked pleadingly at the woman beside it. I could find no words. I might have frothed a little, but not aggressively.

'Pico roco,' the woman said smiling, seeing my confusion and terror. 'Son muy ricos' ('they're very good').

We were sitting in La Caleta at the side of the market. We had decided to eat just fish, to stock up on seafood before we crossed the Andes back into meat country. We'd already sampled some of the joys of the cold-water Humboldt current - sea bass, calamares and crab. We'd filled up with several bowls of the universal Chilean favourite caldillo de congrio, conger eel stew.

I had another bowl of conger eel and asked about the pico roco. Jo said it meant 'rocky beak' and the waitress said 'muy rico.' They were served with soup or cold with mayo. I had both. The beaks were still there. The flesh, the muscle under the diaphragm, was thick and pink like the flesh of a big lobster claw. It tasted like strong crab meat.

It was the ugliest creature I had ever seen and one of the most delicious.

Hank Wangford, **Lost Cowboys**

Rábalo Guisado en Leche de Coco
Bass in Coconut Milk
Colombia

> 5 fillets bass or any non-oily firm fleshed white fish
> 50ml/4 tablespoons olive oil
> 1 onion, finely chopped
> 1 sweet green pepper, seeded and chopped
> 1 jalapeño chilli, seeded and chopped
> 2 green plantains, peeled and cut into 1cm/1/2 inch slices

350ml/12 fl oz coconut milk made from creamed coconut
120ml/4 fl oz thick coconut milk
Salt
45g/3 tablespoons coriander leaves, chopped (optional)

In a large frying pan heat the olive oil and fry the fish until it is lightly golden on both sides. Lift out and set aside. In the oil remaining in the pan add the onion, green pepper, chilli and tomatoes and sauté until the vegetables are tender. Add the plantains, season with salt and pour in the thin coconut milk. Simmer, over low heat for 15 minutes or until the plantains are tender. Add the fish and cook for 5-8 minutes or until the fish is cooked. Pour in the thick coconut milk and sprinkle with the coriander, if liked. *Serves 6.*

Moqueca de Camarão
Bahian Shrimp Stew
BRAZIL

5 tablespoons olive oil
1 large onion, finely chopped
1 medium carrot, scraped and thinly sliced
1 sweet green pepper, seeded and chopped
1 sweet red pepper, seeded and chopped
450 g/1 lb tomatoes, peeled, seeded and chopped
Salt, freshly ground pepper
900 g/2 lb large raw prawns, shelled
2 tablespoons dendê (palm) oil

Heat the olive oil in a large, heavy frying pan and sauté the onion, carrots and both peppers until the vegetables are soft.

Add the tomatoes, stir to mix and season to taste with salt and pepper. Cook until the mixture is well blended, about 5 minutes. Add the prawns and the dendê oil and cook, turning the prawns once or twice for about 3 minutes or until they have turned pink and lost their translucent look. Be careful not to overcook as prawns toughen rapidly. Have ready a warmed platter with a generous border of hot, plainly cooked white rice. Pile the prawns into the centre. Serve with a hot fresh chilli sauce. *Serves 6.*

Ode to Conger Chowder

In the storm-tossed
Chilean
sea
lives the rosy conger,
giant eel
of snowy flesh.
And in Chilean
stewpots,
along the coast,
was born the chowder,
thick and succulent,
a boon to man.
You bring the conger, skinned,
to the kitchen
(its mottled skin slips off
like a glove,
leaving the
grape of the sea
exposed to the world),
naked,
the tender eel
glistens,
prepared
to serve our appetites.
Now
you take
garlic,
first, caress
that precious
ivory,
smell
its irate fragrance,
then
blend the minced garlic
with onion
and tomato
until the onion
is the color of gold.

Meanwhile
steam
our regal
ocean prawns,
and when
they are
tender,
when the savor is
set in a sauce
combining the liquors
of the ocean
and the clear water
released from the light of the onion,
then
you add the eel
that it may be immersed in glory,
that it may be steeped in the oils
of the pot,
shrink and be saturated.
Now all that remains is to
drop a dollop of cream
into the concoction,
a heavy rose,
then slowly
deliver
the treasure to the flame,
until in the chowder
are warmed
the essences of Chile,
and to the table
come, newly wed,
the savors
of land and sea,
that in this dish
you may know heaven.

PABLO NERUDA, **Elemental Odes**

MEAT AND POULTRY

MEAT AND POULTRY

Before the Spanish conquest, the Americas had few domesticated, edible animals. In Mexico the Aztecs raised turkeys; in Peru the Inca bred *cuy* (guinea pig - pronounced kwee). There were also ducks, doves, quail and pheasants (the curassow). Wild boar (the peccary) was hunted and deer were raised in some regions of Peru and Mexico. In the Andes there were the cameloid animals, llamas, alpaca, vicuña, guanaco and so on which had been domesticated for so long that there was no trace of the wild ancestors. Though used as a beast of burden and for its wool, the llama was also used to make *charqui* (dried meat), corrupted to *jerky* in the USA where dried beef is the ingredient.

Latin America also had a large number of rodents, rabbit-like animals of varying size, from the small *agouti* still eaten in Argentina, to the middle-sized *paca* and *viscacha*, and the giant *capybara*, a great water lover often found basking on rocks on river banks. A colleague told me that early Christian missionaries, finding it good to eat, reclassified it as a type of fish that could be indulged in on fast days. The Spanish, and to a lesser extent the Portuguese, introduced sheep, goats, cattle and pigs. The pigs were much preferred to the wild, lean and wily creatures indigenous to the continent. The domestic hen was also introduced. Meat and poultry dishes of the post-conquest era are, therefore, colonial, resulting from a true culinary wedding of Old and New Worlds.

At the time of the conquest, Spanish cuisine was strongly influenced by Arab culture, as reflected in the inclusion of meat and nuts in some meat dishes. The use of nuts as a thickening agent depended on the different nuts available. *Pepitas* (pumpkin seeds), peanuts, cashews, pecans and Brazil nuts had probably always been used in the Americas but almonds and walnuts were introduced from Europe. *Albóndigas*, meat balls, were adopted and adapted with a complex pattern of influences: Old World domesticated animals and cooking patterns allied with New World foods like the capsicums (sweet, pungent and hot), the tomato, the potato, familiar and unfamiliar seasonings, annatto (achiote) and allspice. Newcomers also included cinnamon, cloves and nutmeg, olive oil with the New World, corn and peanut oils and much later from Africa, dendê (palm) oil.

In the Caribbean, English-speaking islands such as Jamaica and St Kitts created a marinade they called seasoning-up. Spanish speakers call it sofrito. There are no precise recipes but a good seasoning-up would include some of the following: garlic, local chives, onion, thyme, marjoram, chillies, sweet peppers, parsley, celery leaves, peppercorns, Worcestershire sauce, sage, brown sugar, sugar, tomato ketchup, rum and vinegar.

In the Argentinian Carbonada Criolla, Old World beef combines with new world vegetables such as pumpkin (winter squash), courgettes (zucchini), peppers, tomatoes, sweet potatoes, potatoes and corn. Conversely, vegetables previously unknown in the Americas, the green immigrants from Europe such as cabbage and green peas, appear in many of the continent's meat and poultry dishes, along with onion, garlic, and eggplant (aubergine). Likewise, plantation dishes like *sancochos* are an interesting medley of vegetables from both worlds. Lacking wheat flour to make pastry, Bolivians created a delicious corn topping for a chicken pie. In Chile, the potato, another American native vegetable, was used as a topping for a meat pie similar to shepherd's pie, while Argentinian cooks have adapted the European technique of cooking meat in milk.

An entertaining example of what can happen to dishes when they go on their travels is *Pollo con Arroz* (chicken with rice), a simplified form of Paella. While Paella is thought of as purely Spanish, Pollo con Arroz is universally accepted and loved as a dish that belongs in all of Latin America. It turns up, slightly altered, in the English-speaking island of Barbados as Fowl Down-in-Rice, this time with a tomato sauce cooked separately and poured over the finished dish. Onions, garlic, sweet peppers, tomatoes, and sometimes chillies, saffron and annato are among the usual ingredients. When cooks prefer a more elaborate dish, they add chopped ham, raisins, olives and capers. For the most part, however, it is safe to say the dish has migrated with its essentials of chicken and rice unchanged. There is a Filipino rice and chicken soup that comes from Spain but perhaps the most exotic variation is in the Puerto Rican *Asopao de Pollo*, a chicken and rice stew.

All over Latin America there are examples of one of the oldest forms of cooking: the neolithic oven. It varies from country to country in detail though not in essentials and has maintained its popularity over the centuries. Today it is especially used to prepare holiday food. In Chile it is called the *curanto* and like the clambake of New England, seaweed is used to line the 'oven' which is a pit lined with hot rocks. The feast is a lavish affair, including the magnificent seafood of the region: lobsters, prawns, crabs, oysters, mussels. There is often a whole suckling pig as well, and vegetables such as peas, green beans and special potato cakes.

In Peru the oven is called a *pachamanca* from the Quechua words for earth and oven. It is a very grand affair. The pit is dug, wood is burned down to heat the stones and the pit is then lined with moist greenery and aromatic herbs, followed by the food which might be a kid (baby goat), *cuyes* (guinea pigs), a suckling pig, chickens, or whatever is available. Then there are casseroles of rice with corn, potatoes, sweet potatoes, various vegetables and, of course, chillies (called *ají* in Peru). When all the foods have been accommodated, the hole is covered with more greenery and hot stones, then the pit is sealed with more earth. As this is holiday food, the mound of earth is often decorated with flowers. About six hours later when the food has finished cooking, the pit is opened and the feast begins with singing, dancing and usually a good deal of drinking.

Just as seaweed lends a subtle flavour to the Chilean *curanto*, aromatic herbs add flavour to the Mexican earth oven which is called a *barbacoa*. The word, barbacoa, comes from the Taino Indian word for a framework of branches for sleeping on or for drying meat. The barbacoa is lined with *pencas de maguey* (agave leaves), which give subtle overtones of flavour reminiscent of tequila. The barbacoa is a favourite in and around Mexico City where barbacoa restaurants are common. A ranch-owning friend regularly gives a barbacoa for family and friends. It begins the day before the party with the slaughter of a young lamb, skinned and dressed and cut into sections. Next day the pit is dug and the sides plastered with mud to keep them stable. The pit is then filled with stones and finally a pile of wood is lit on top to heat them. While the wood is burning, the agave leaves are roasted in the fire until they are limp. Then they are cleaned and used to line the pit, overlapping it on the outside. After the wood has burned down, a large grate is lowered to the bottom and on it is put a big basin or casserole dish with the ingredients for *Consommé de Barbacoa*: rice, carrots, potatoes, cabbage, chick peas, chillies and herbs. An oven rack goes over this and on the rack lies the lamb. The agave leaves are folded down over everything and the pit is sealed and left for 4 - 6 hours when the lamb will be cooked and the soup basin filled with juices from the lamb. Drinks, sauces, tortillas and guacamole are on hand as the feast begins.

The *pib* of Mexico's Yucatán peninsula is prepared in a similar fashion to a barbacoa but with some variations. It is lined with banana leaves which gives it a distinct flavour and a suckling pig is the favourite meat rather than lamb. Seville orange juice, cumin, garlic, black peppercorns, oregano and achiote are used to make a marinade and the pig is marinaded until it is time to cook. A large dish is lined with banana leaves, the pig placed on top with the marinade poured over it, then the pit is covered in the usual way. After three hours the suckling pig will be cooked, the pit is opened and the feast begins with beer, tortillas and sauces to accompany it.

Another sort of barbecue is the Argentinian *asado criollo* which originated with Argentinian cowboys, the *gauchos*. Similarly, in the cattle region of Rio Grande do Sul in Brazil, there is a barbecue form of cooking called a *Churrasco a Gaúcha*. Here, as in Argentina, whole carcasses are spitted on long iron skewers stuck in the soil at an angle to the fire. Today most people find a barbecue pit with a grate more convenient for family or backyard barbecues. In Argentinian and Brazilian barbecue restaurants (the Brazilian version is called a *churrascaria*) meats and poultry are cooked on wall-sized grills.

MEAT AND POULTRY

Chivito Adobado
Kid in Adobo Sauce
ARGENTINA

Kid, sometimes called baby goat, is a Latin American favourite, especially in mountainous or dry regions, and especially in northern Mexico and in Bolivia. This recipe came originally from Argentina.

900 g/2 lb kid, cut into serving pieces
1 onion, thinly sliced
2 cloves garlic, chopped
5g/1 teaspoon dried thyme, crumbled
10g/2 teaspoons dried oregano, crumbled
1 bay leaf, broken up
Salt, freshly ground pepper
120ml/4 fl oz oil, (corn, peanut or olive oil)
250ml/8 fl oz dry white wine
120ml/4 fl oz chicken or beef stock

Rinse the kid and pat it dry with paper towels. In a bowl mix together the onion, garlic, thyme, oregano, bay leaf and salt and pepper (adobo sauce see page 81). Mix the seasonings with the kid and put them into a dish. Pour in the oil, cover with the dish and refrigerate it overnight. Strain the oil into a flameproof casserole and sauté the kid pieces, with the adobo for a few minutes. Add the wine and stock, cover and cook over low heat until the kid is tender, 1 1/2 to 2 hours. Lift out the kid to a warm serving dish, strain the sauce and pour it over. Serve with mashed potatoes and any cooked vegetables or salad. *Serves 4-6.*

Pollo Guisado con Coco
Chicken in Coconut Milk
GUATEMALA

1.5kg/3 lb chicken, cut into serving pieces
45ml/3 tablespoons corn oil
1 onion, finely chopped
2 cloves garlic, chopped
2 sweet red peppers, seeded and chopped
225g/8 oz tomatoes, peeled and chopped
30g/2 tablespoons coriander sprigs, chopped
5g/1 teaspoon ground annatto (achiote)
Salt
475ml/16 fl oz thin coconut milk.

In a frying pan heat the oil and sauté the chicken pieces until they are lightly golden all over. Lift out to a flameproof casserole. In the oil remaining in the frying pan sauté the onion, garlic and sweet red peppers until they are soft. Add the tomatoes and cook, stirring from time to time, until the mixture is well blended. Stir in the coriander and annatto and pour over the chicken. Mix creamed coconut to the consistency of milk and add 475ml/16 fl oz to the chicken. Season with salt. Cover and simmer over moderate heat until the chicken is tender, about 45 minutes. Lift out the chicken to a platter, cover and keep warm. Reduce the sauce over brisk heat, stirring, until reduced and thickened. Pour over the chicken. Serve with rice. *Serves 6.*

For each meal his servants prepared him more than thirty dishes cooked in their native style, which they put over small earthenware braziers to prevent them from getting cold. They cooked more than three hundred plates of the food the great Moctezuma was going to eat, and more than a thousand more for the guard. I have heard that they used to cook him the flesh of young boys. But as he had such a variety of dishes, made of so many different ingredients, we could not tell whether a dish was of human flesh or anything else, since every day they cooked fowls, turkeys, pheasants, local partridges, quail, tame and wild duck, venison, wild boar, marsh birds, pigeons, hares and rabbits, also many other kinds of birds and beasts native to their country, so numerous that I cannot quickly name them all. I know for certain, however, that after our Captain spoke against the sacrifice of human beings and the eating of their flesh, Moctezuma ordered that it should no longer be served to him.

Let us now turn to the way his meals were served, which was like this. If it was cold, they built a large fire of live coals made by burning the bark of a tree which gave off no smoke. The smell of the bark from which they made these coals was very sweet. In order that he should get no more heat than he wanted, they placed a sort of screen in front of it adorned with the figures of idols worked in gold. He would sit on a soft, low stool, which was richly worked. His table, which was also low and decorated in the same way, was covered with white tablecloths and rather long napkins of the same material. Then four very clean and beautiful girls brought water for his hands in one of those deep basins that they call *xicales*. They held others like plates beneath it to catch the water, and brought him towels. Two other women brought him maize-cakes.

When he began his meal they placed in front of him a sort of wooden screen, richly decorated with gold, so that no one should see him eat. Then the four women retired, and four great chieftains, all old men, stood beside him. He talked with them every now and again and asked some questions, and as a great favour he would sometimes offer one of them a dish of whatever tasted best. They say that these were his closest relations and advisers and judges of lawsuits, and if he gave them anything to eat they ate it standing, with deep reverence and without looking in his face.

BERNAL DÍAZ DEL CASTILLO, **The Conquest of New Spain**

Carne Frita
Shredded Beef
VENEZUELA

Venezuela is beef country and this recipe has echoes of the Spanish past and the oddly named *Ropa Vieja* (Old Clothes) a shredded beef dish. Tomatoes, peppers and chilli are new world contributions.

    900g/2 lbs flank steak in one piece
    Beef stock, about 475ml/16 fl oz cups
    45ml/3 tablespoons corn oil
    1 onion, chopped
    2 cloves garlic, chopped
    2 sweet red peppers, seeded and chopped
    1.5g/1/4 teaspoon ground cumin
    5g/1 teaspoon hot paprika
    Salt, freshly ground pepper

Put the beef into a flameproof casserole and pour in enough stock to cover it. Bring to a simmer, cover and cook over low heat until it is tender, about 2 hours. Cool in the stock. Remove the beef and shred it, cover and set aside. Reserve the stock.

Heat the oil in a large frying pan and sauté the onion, garlic and red peppers until they are soft. Add the tomatoes, cumin, paprika, salt and pepper and cook for 5 minutes longer, until the mixture is thick and well blended. Stir in the reserved shredded beef and about 120ml/4 fl oz of the stock and simmer for 5 minutes longer to blend the flavours. Taste for seasoning and add more hot paprika, if liked. Serve with rice. *Serves 6.*

Cochifrito
Lamb with Seasonings
URUGUAY

The original of this dish came from Aragon in Spain, but changed considerably on its way to Uruguay where I met it. It is found in Latin America wherever good lamb is to be found.

    120ml/4 fl oz olive oil
    900 g/2 lb lean boneless lamb cut into 2.5cm/1 inch pieces
    2 onions, chopped
    3 cloves garlic, chopped
    30g/2 tablespoons flat parsley, chopped
    Salt, freshly ground pepper
    2 slices white bread, toasted
    250ml/8 fl oz chicken or beef stock
    30ml/2 tablespoons mild white vinegar

Heat the oil in a flameproof casserole, and add the lamb pieces. Sauté the lamb until it is golden, lift it out with a slotted spoon and set it aside. Add the onions and garlic and as soon as the onion is soft return the lamb together with the seasonings, and the stock. Cover and cook over low heat until half cooked. Moisten the toast with the vinegar, add it to the casserole and gently break it up. Cook, uncovered, still over very low heat until the lamb is tender, and the sauce is smooth. *Serves 6.*

M y day begins at four in the morning, especially when my compañero is on the first shift. I prepare his breakfast. Then I have to prepare the *salteñas* (a Bolivian small pie, filled with meat, potatoes, hot pepper, and other spices) because I make about one hundred salteñas every day and I sell them in the street. I do this in order to make up for what my husband doesn't cover in terms of our necessities. The night before, we prepare the dough and at four in the morning I make the salteñas while I feed the kids. The kids help me: they peel potatoes and carrots and make the dough.

Then the ones that go to school in the morning have to get ready, while I wash the clothes I left soaking overnight. At eight I go out to sell. The kids that go to school in the afternoon help me. We have to go to the company store and bring home the staples. And in the store there are immensely long lines and you have to wait there until eleven in order to stock up. You have to line up for meat, for vegetables, for oil. So it's just one line after another. Since everything's in a different place, that's how it has to be. So all the time I'm selling salteñas, I line up to buy my supplies at the store. I run up to the counter to get the things and the kids sell. Then the kids line up and I sell. That's how we do it.

DOMITILA BARRIOS DE CHUNGARA with MOEMA VIEZZER, **Let Me Speak! Testimony of Domitila, a Woman of the Bolivian Mines**

Viscacha a la Casserola
Casseroled Viscacha
ARGENTINA

This is a small rabbit-like creature I enjoyed in Buenos Aires. I find rabbit a more than adequate substitute.

> 900g/2 lb rabbit, cut into serving pieces
> 2 onions, sliced
> 2 cloves garlic, chopped
> 750ml/1 1/4 pints dry red wine
> Salt, freshly ground pepper
> 30g/2 tablespoons chopped flat parsley
> 60ml/4 tablespoons olive oil
> 450g/1 lb tomatoes, peeled and chopped
> 15g/1 tablespoon sweet paprika

Put the rabbit pieces into a flameproof casserole and cover with the onions, garlic, season with salt and pepper and add the parsley. Pour in the wine, set in a cool place, lightly covered and marinate for 8 hours, or refrigerate, if liked. Heat the oil in a large frying pan. Lift out and pat the rabbit pieces dry and sauté until lightly browned all over. Add the tomatoes and paprika and cook for 5 minutes longer. Strain the marinade. Return the solids to the casserole with 250ml/8 fl oz of the wine and reserve the rest of the wine for another use. Add the rabbit and the contents of the frying pan to the casserole, cover and cook over low heat until the rabbit is tender, about 2 hours. The time will vary according to the age of the rabbit. Serve with the sauce and potatoes. *Serves 4.*

Carne Asada
Roast Beef
CUBA

> 1.5kg/3 lb topside of beef or similar cut in 1 piece
> 45ml/3 tablespoons lemon juice
> 2.5g/1/2 teaspoon dried thyme, crumbled
> 2 cloves garlic, crushed
> 30g/2 tablespoons chopped coriander sprigs
> Freshly ground pepper to taste
> 60ml/4 tablespoons olive oil
> 1 sweet red pepper, seeded and chopped
> 2 onions, thinly sliced
> 475ml/16 fl oz beef stock
> Salt

Mix together the thyme, garlic, coriander, garlic and a generous amount of freshly ground black pepper. Rub the mixture into the beef and put it into a container in the refrigerator overnight. Pat the beef dry and sauté the pepper and onion, adding a little more oil if necessary. Add to the casserole together with any marinade and the beef stock. Bring to a simmer, cover and cook over low heat for 2 hours, or until the beef is tender. Lift the beef out to a warm platter and reduce the sauce over brisk heat. Slice and serve the beef with the sauce and vegetables, such as potatoes or green vegetables. *Serves 6-8.*

Lomo de Cerdo Dulce
Sweet Loin of Pork
PERU

> 50g/2 ozsugar
> Salt
> 1.4kg/3 lb boneless pork loin in one piece
> 250ml/8 fl oz dry white wine
> 120ml/4 fl oz milk
> 50g/2 oz/4 tablespoons butter, melted

1 clove
1.5g/¹/4 teaspoon ground cinnamon
115g/4 oz seedless raisins
30ml/2 tablespoons soft breadcrumbs

Season the pork with the sugar and salt and put it into a flameproof casserole. Pour in the wine, cover and marinate for 12 hours. At the end of the time add the melted butter, clove, cinnamon and raisins. Sprinkle in the breadcrumbs and cook, covered, on top of the stove for about 2½ hours, or until the pork is tender. If liked, the pork can be roasted in the oven in which case it should be basted every hour or so. *Serves 6-8.*

Pollo Borracho
Drunken Chicken
Colombia

I first enjoyed this in Colombia, but it is a favourite family dish in many countries and wherever wine is produced.

30ml/2 tablespoons butter or lard
1.5kg/3 lb chicken, cut into serving pieces

Salt, freshly ground pepper
2 whole cloves
2.5cm/1 inch piece stick cinnamon, broken in half
2.5g/1/2 teaspoon ground cumin
2 cloves garlic, chopped
225g/8 oz boiled ham, cut into 1 cm/1/2 inch strips
250ml/8 fl oz dry white wine
50ml/2 fl oz mild white vinegar
For garnish, pitted green olives and capers

Grease a flameproof casserole with the butter or lard. Arrange the chicken legs on the bottom. Season with salt and pepper, the garlic and half the spices and top with half the ham. Pour on half the wine and half the vinegar and make another layer using the chicken breasts. Cover and cook over a low heat until the chicken is tender, 45 minutes to one hour. Arrange the chicken and ham on a platter, nap with the sauce and garnish with the olives and capers. *Serves 6.*

L as Pampas was twenty miles on from Río Pico, the last settlement before the frontier. To the north towered El Cono, an extinct volcano of bone-white screes and brighter snows. In the valley the river ran fast and green over white stones. Each log cabin had a potato patch, barricaded from cattle by stakes and thorns.

There were two families at Las Pampas, Patrocinio and Solís. Each accused the other of cattle-stealing, but both hated the State logging company and in their hatred they were friends.

It was Sunday. God had given a son to the Patrocinio who owned the bar and he was celebrating the event with an *asado*. Riders had been coming in for two days. Their horses were hitched in the stable, their lariats and boleadoras tucked into the girths. The men lay in white clover, drinking wine from skins and warming themselves by the fire. The sun dispersed the milky haze that hung in patches over the valley.

Rolf Mayer, a gaucho with German and Italian blood, did the butchery. He was lean and silent with mighty scarlet hands. He was dressed all over in chocolate brown and never took off his hat. He had a knife made from a bayonet with a yellow ivory pommel. He laid each sheep on a trestle and began undressing the carcass until it lay, pink and sheeny, legs in the air, on the white inner lining of its own fleece. Then he slipped the knife point in where the skin stretches tight over the belly and the hot blood spurted over his hands. He enjoyed that. You could tell he enjoyed it by the way he lowered his eyelids and stuck out his lower lip and sucked the air in through his teeth. He pulled out the guts, skimmed them of liver and kidneys and threw the rest to the dogs.

He carried the five carcasses to the fire and crucified each one to its iron cross, set on an incline to the flame.

BRUCE CHATWIN, **In Patagonia**

Lomo de Cerdo a la Caucana
Pork Loin in Milk
ARGENTINA

900 g/2 lbs pork loin, boned
1.1 litres/2 pts whole milk
50 ml/2 fl oz fresh lemon juice
1 onion, finely chopped
1 clove garlic, chopped
3 tablespoons unsalted butter
Salt, freshly ground pepper

Put the pork into a casserole or ovenproof baking dish that will hold it comfortably and pour over it the milk and lemon juice mixed together. Cover with a cloth and leave overnight in a cool place. When ready to cook lift the pork out of the milk mixture and pat it dry with paper towels. Season with salt and pepper. In a frying pan heat the butter and sauté the pork until it is very lightly browned all over. Lift the pork back into the dish with the milk mixture. In the butter remaining in the pan sauté the onion and garlic until the onion is soft. Add the contents of the frying pan to the baking dish scraping up any pan drippings. Bake the pork, uncovered, in a preheated 180°C/350°F oven for about 2 hours or until the pork is tender.

Lift the pork out onto a warmed serving platter and remove any string tying it. Cover and keep warm. Skim any fat from the sauce. Reduce it over brisk heat to 350 ml/12 fl oz stirring from time to time. Taste for seasoning and add a little salt if necessary. The sauce will be rather grainy in texture. Slice the pork and serve the sauce separately. Serve hot with rice and a green vegetable. The pork is also good cold with salad. *Serves 6.*

Pollo Almendrado Rojo
Red Chicken with Almonds
MEXICO

1.6 kg/3 1/2 lb chicken cut into serving pieces
3 tablespoons olive oil
450 ml/16 fl oz chicken stock
1 sprig thyme
1 tablespoon coriander sprigs
1 onion, finely chopped
2 cloves garlic, chopped
1 small fresh red chilli, seeded and chopped, or more to taste
450 g/1 lb tomatoes, peeled, seeded and chopped
125 g/4 oz finely ground almonds
125 ml/2 fl oz dry sherry

Pat the chicken pieces dry with paper towels. Heat the oil in large, heavy skillet and sauté the chicken pieces until golden on both sides. Lift the chicken pieces out to a casserole, pour in the chicken stock, thyme and coriander sprigs and simmer, covered, over low heat until the chicken is tender, about 45 minutes. Lift out the chicken and strain the stock. Discard the herbs and return the chicken and stock to the casserole.

In the oil remaining in the skillet sauté the onion, garlic, chilli and tomatoes until the onion is soft. Transfer to a food processor with the almonds and purée, adding a little of the chicken stock if needed. Pour the sauce over the chicken, taste for salt, and simmer to thicken the sauce and heat through. Stir in the sherry and serve. *Serves 6.*

Luciano, who was acting as kitchen aid to Rodrigo, took the turkeys - it was almost dark - salted them, and gave them back to Rodrigo, who put them on to cook - an aroma I can still remember. The rest of the troop - in camp we put the rain cover up in a circle - sat down in the center to talk and joke around, in the same place where we always stood for formation. 'What are they doing in the city?' we wondered. Rodrigo said we could sing, and we did.

After singing a while we had to go pee. When you left the group to go to pee, you thought immediately of the city, your family, your mom, your girl, our chances for victory. How many more Christmases, how long would this all go on, when could we go back home? All that in the instant you went off to pee. But back in the group again and singing and kidding around, you forgot all about it. While we were chatting, Rodrigo was cooking. Aroma after aroma began to float out from the kitchen area as one by one Rodrigo tossed in the seasonings. And one by one the familiar sounds came back to us - capers, catsup, Worcestershire sauce, mustard. We were 20 yards from the kitchen, but the wind was blowing, and these were such familiar smells. Our senses, our sense perceptions, had grown sharper, and we recognized the spices. 'What was that one?' we asked. 'That's it!' And so on...

Finally, the call we'd all been waiting for, in that usual tone between firm and noncommital, firm and mechanical, firm and dry: 'Time to eat, compañeros!' We all got in line. And that mouth-watering smell! First, I touched the food with my fingers, in the dark, not with my spoon but with my fingers. I remember I touched the olives, the capers. In the dark by touch you recognise all the different ingredients. I took an olive and chomped into it. It made me think of olives in the city - the olive juice or your saliva mixed with the olive produces an ecstatic sensation that takes you back to the city...

But then came the great tragedy, with a whole shitload of curses flung at Luciano, and Rodrigo's fury, and the demoralisation of everybody: the meat had come already salted, but Luciano had put more salt on top of that, and it was inedible!

OMAR CABEZAS, **Fire from the Mountain: the Making of a Sandinista**

Pepián de Pollo
Chicken in Pumpkin Seed Sauce
GUATEMALA

>1.6 kg/3¹/2 lb chicken, cut into serving pieces
>450 ml/16 fl oz chicken stock
>125 g/4 oz Mexican pumpkin seeds (pepitas)
>3 large sweet red peppers, seeded and coarsely chopped
>450 g/1 lb tomatoes, peeled and chopped
>1 onion, chopped
>3 cloves garlic, chopped
>2 tablespoons corn oil
>125 ml/4 fl oz fresh orange juice
>¹/4 teaspoon ground allspice
>Salt, freshly ground pepper
>
>Garnish (optional)
>40 g/1 ¹/2 oz seedless raisins
>Butter
>25 g/1 oz slivered almonds

Arrange the chicken pieces in a large, heavy casserole and pour in the chicken stock. Cover and cook over very low heat until almost tender, about 30 minutes. In a nut grinder or food processor grind the pumpkin seeds as finely as possible and shake through a sieve. Set aside. In a food processor combine the peppers, tomatoes, onion and garlic and reduce to a purée. Transfer to a bowl and stir in the pumpkin seeds. In a skillet heat the oil, stir in the purée and cook over moderate heat, stirring constantly, for 5 minutes. Drain the chicken, reserving the stock, and return to the casserole. Stir 225 ml/8 fl oz of the reserved stock, the orange juice, allspice, salt and pepper into the purée and pour the mixture over the chicken. Cover and cook over very low heat until the chicken is tender, about 15 minutes. Soak the raisins in warm water for a few minutes if using, and sauté the almonds in a little butter until they are golden. Transfer the chicken to a serving dish and sprinkle with the raisins and almonds. Serve with plainly cooked rice. *Serves 6.*

Pollo a la Paisana
Country-style Chicken
CHILE

>1.5kg/3 lb chicken, quartered
>3 onions, sliced thinly
>4 cloves garlic, left whole
>30g/2 tablespoons flat parsley sprigs, chopped
>Salt, freshly ground pepper
>60ml/4 tablespoons olive oil
>30ml/2 tablespoons mild vinegar

Put the chicken pieces in a flameproof casserole with the legs at the bottom, the breast quarters on top. Top the chicken with the onions, garlic and parsley. Season with salt and pepper. Mix the oil and vinegar together and pour into the casserole. Cover and cook over low heat until the chicken is tender, 45 minutes to one hour. Serve with fried potatoes and a green salad or watercress salad. *Serves 4.*

Outside in an overflow market we saw an old Indian woman selling iguanas. They were cheap; you could buy a miniature dragon with three feet of whip-lash tail, all alive, for twenty or thirty cents. Flayed and gutted, the dried carcasses of several more lay in a neat row on the pavement, a pale meat crusty with flies. Near them stood an enormous bowl, full of iguana eggs. Curiosity wrestled with prejudice and was at last defeated; we moved away, leaving the eggs untasted. That evening we happened to pass along the same street. Business in lizards had evidently been slack; the old woman's pitch was still crawling with monsters. While we were looking, she began to pack up her wares for the night. One by one, she took up the animals and dumped them into a circular basket. The tails projected, writhing. Angrily she shoved them back into place; but while one was being folded away, another would spring out, and then another. It was like a battle with the hydra. The abhorred tails were finally confined under a net. Then, hoisting the lizards on to her head, and with the bowl of their eggs under her arm, the old woman marched away, muttering...

ALDOUS HUXLEY, **Beyond the Mexique Bay**

VEGETABLES AND SALAD

VEGETABLES
AND SALAD

On arrival in the Americas, the conquerors found a wealth of vegetables unknown to them. Bernal Díaz del Castillo, a captain with Hernán Cortés and author of *La Historia Verdadera de la Conquista de la Nueva España* (The True History of the Conquest of New Spain), wrote of his great delight and astonishment on visiting the Tianguis, the great market of Tenochtitlán, capital of the Aztecs and now modern Mexico City. I have the same feeling of delight when visiting markets in Latin America today. The heaps of red, green, yellow, and orange peppers (called *ajíes* in South America) and the ripe red abundance of tomatoes in the market in Guadalajara in Mexico still kindle that sense of excitement.

Probably corn (maize) was the most important of the vegetables originating in the Americas because of its profound agricultural and nutritional consequences worldwide (see Corn). From the culinary point of view, the tomato is the fruit which we would least like to be without. As well as the true tomato, there is the small green husk tomato (*Physalis ixocarpa*), also Mexican in origin. The capsicum peppers, sweet, pungent and hot, may be the greatest gift of all to the cookpots and salad bowls of the world. Peppers spread worldwide with astonishing rapidity. Botanically they are *Capsicum annum* and *Capsicum frutescence* of the *Solanaceae* family to which tomatoes, potatoes and aubergines also belong. Believed to have been cultivated in the Valley of Mexico as early as 7000 BC, and unknown outside the Americas until the arrival of Columbus, they are known in Nahuatl (the language of the Aztecs) as *chilli* and are still known by this name in many parts of the world. The Spanish changed the name to *chile*. Other types of peppers were cultivated in Peru where they are called *ajíes*. Although these are tremendously popular throughout the South American continent, they have not spread worldwide like the chillies. There are an estimated one hundred varieties of peppers, each with a different taste, shape, colour and size.

Roughly speaking, when they are green (unripe) they are used fresh or pickled, and when ripe they are used dried. There are, of course, some exceptions like the *pimientos*. This Spanish favourite is a sweet red pepper, widely popular everywhere and used by the Hungarians to make paprika. There are six varieties of sweet red peppers, ranging from the mild but delicate Noble Sweet paprika through the rose paprika to the hot type.

A much used green chilli is the small *serrano*, often pickled (en escabeche) but also sold fresh, canned or bottled in supermarkets. The fresh ripe (red) chilli is less frequently used. It is added as a condiment by those liking hot food and in sauces, salads and in Mexican *tacos*. Vying with the serrano in popularity is the *jalapeño*. Larger and with more flavour, it is a favourite whenever a touch of heat is wanted, such as in *guacamole* or the corn dishes. It is widely available pickled and bottled. The *poblano*, very dark, almost black green, larger than the jalapeño and very flavourful, is not readily found outside Mexico and North America. It is of varying hotness, often served cut into strips and fried to accompany meats. The poblano pepper is used for *Chiles en Nogado*, the great dish for Independence Day in Mexico when they are stuffed with *picadillo* (meat hash), fried and masked with a fresh walnut sauce and garnished with pomegranate seeds, red, green and white - the colours of the Mexican flag. The best substitute is a large sweet green pepper.

Some of the Mexican peppers change their character dramatically when they ripen from green to red. The poblano when ripe turns into the *ancho*, the pepper most commonly used in Mexico. It is richly flavoured and mild, wrinkled and large measuring about 7.5cm/3 inches by 12.5cm/5 inches. To use it, the seeds are shaken out and the pepper is torn to pieces, soaked in warm water to soften it, then pureed in a food processor and used as the base for a cooked sauce; with the long, slender, dark *pasilla*, which is the ripe, dried *chilaca*, and the wrinkled, very dark brown *mulato*, they are used in the festival dish, *Mole Poblano*.

The *chipotle*, lighter brown and wrinkled with a very exotic flavour, is the ripe jalapeño, dried and smoked. The *guajillo* is smooth-skinned and its redness adds a beautiful colour and flavour to food. Medium-sized, it is sometimes very picante and can be referred to as the naughty chilli because of its bite. Just to confuse matters, it is often mistakenly called the *cascabel* (rattle) because its seeds rattle when it is shaken. The cascabel is small, round and pungent.

Another fresh pepper used green or red is the small lantern-shaped *habañero*, the hottest pepper in North America. It is also known in Guatemala as *chile caballero* (gentleman pepper), and in English as the Scotch Bonnet. I first tasted it in Jamaica when I was at school there for a while. It has a most exquisite flavour, once tasted never forgotten. It will improve almost any dish to which it is added.

The two most popular chillies in South America are the *mirasol* and the *rocoto*. The rocoto is larger, green when immature, and can be yellow, orange or red when ripe. Especially popular in Bolivia, where it is called *locoto*, it seems to be eaten with almost everything. The mirasol, a beautiful yellow pepper of medium size and long rather than wide, is probably better known as *ají amarillo* (yellow pepper). Its Quechua name is *kellu-uchu* and when dried it is called *cusqueño*, meaning from Cuzco. Like other South American peppers it is very hot and not to be confused with the mirasol from Mexico which is a guajillo. Mirasol means 'looking at the sun'.

The potato, *Solanum tuberosum*, is called papa in Aymara, the language of the first people to cultivate it in the high Andes of what are now Peru and Bolivia. Potatoes may have been cultivated from as early as 8000 BC and undoubtedly since 3000 BC. There are a great many types such as the large yellow-fleshed (not sweet) ones, small yellow *criollos* which don't disintegrate when cooked, purple-fleshed ones and, of course, white ones. In the Andes, a primitive form of freeze drying was invented which is still practised today. The potatoes are put out in the cold Andean night where they freeze. When they thaw in the early morning sunshine, the liquid is trampled out of them. After three days they are quite dry and like stone. They keep indefinitely and when soaked, they are as good as new, except that the flesh is black. These are called *chuno* and I have done some myself using a modern freezer and the summer sun to prove that the technique works. I never mastered the technique for *tunta*, however, where the potatoes stay white.

There are a number of excellent and unusual recipes for potatoes, especially in Peru, Colombia and Ecuador. My favourite is the Peruvian *Ocopa Arequipeña*, garnished potatoes with a cheese and walnut sauce. It makes a good luncheon dish that is also vegetarian. There are many versions and some cooks make it non-vegetarian by adding prawns. Peruvians like their food fiery and it is wise to adjust the amount of ají to personal taste. There is a potato soup still popular in the region that has the same name as the original dish, *locro*, though the modern dish has imported ingredients like milk, cream and cheese. Another is *chupe*, a dish that is almost a meal in itself with potatoes, eggs and often seafood.

The sweet potato, botanically *Ipomea batata*, is another native of South America, though it is not related to the potato. The sweet potato may have been cultivated as early as 2500 BC. Its skin colour may be reddish-brown, pink or white and the flesh varies from deep orange through to yellow and white. The type with brown skin and moist, sweet, orange yellow flesh is known as the Louisiana yam in the USA, though in fact yams are members of a different botanical group, the *Diocoreas*, and they are legion. The preferred sweet potato of Latin America is the white-fleshed sweet potato called *boniato*. It is much drier than other kinds. A number of yams are also cultivated in Latin America. In Brazil, the most popular root vegetable is *manioc* (cassava). Toasted cassava meal, known as *farofa,* is sprinkled on Brazilian dishes in the same way we use salt and pepper. Squashes, pumpkins and courgettes originated in the Americas too.

The common bean, *Phaseolus vulgaris*, is believed to have been cultivated in Mexico as early as 5000 BC. It is one of the Americas' greatest contributions to the world's kitchen. These days, the kidney or haricot bean is the most widely used bean in the Americas. This bean is either white, red, pink, pinto (speckled), or black. Lima beans (*Phaseolus lunatus*) originated in South America and are now popular in many parts of the world. The broad bean (*Vicia faba*) from the Middle East is eaten a good deal in Latin America where it is called *fava*, and another import that is equally used is the chickpea (*Cicer arietinum*), known as *garbanzo*. There is also the yard-long bean (*Vigna sesquí pedalís*), more of a curiosity than anything else, but used in the Caribbean, and the cranberry bean consumed in Chile. The scarlet runner bean originated in Mexico and is still esteemed in many countries for its showy red flowers, as well as for its edible pods and beans.

Latin American bean dishes are endless. A Cuban one from Spain called *Moros y Cristianos* (Moors and Christians) in which rice and black beans are combined, crops up all over the region in altered forms. Black haricot beans are used in soups throughout the region (see Soups) and are particularly popular in

Brazil where they are the key ingredient of Brazil's national dish *Fejoada Completa*. Brazil is said to be the largest bean-producing country on earth. Black beans are also popular in Central America and in Mexico's Yucatán. Pinto beans are used for Mexican *Frijoles Refritos* (Refried Beans) although the red kidney bean is also acceptable. Beans are served with sauces, cooked with chorizo sausages, mixed with bacon, chillies, tomatoes and fresh coriander, with beer, cheese, eggs and even with sour cream. Sometimes the beans are mashed; other times they are left whole as a brothy or soupy consistency.

Amongst the continent's more original salads is a simple cucumber salad from Bolivia made special by the addition of cubes of ripe papaya, and the Guatemalan *Chojín*, an unusual combination of *chicharrones* (fried pork rinds) and radishes. *Chojín* is sold in Guatemalan markets and is eaten both as a salad and as an appetizer with tortillas. There are innumerable slight variations on the salad. Some versions include tomato, others omit onion. It is one of those traditional dishes where each cook lays claim to the authentic version.

A t the village jetty women are soaking and beating *moriche*. This is the fibre they extract from the *moriche* palm (*Mauritia flexuosa*). This is soaked, beaten and then hung to dry. Hanging on the line to dry, a wad of *moriche* looks alarmingly like a giant helping of Shredded Wheat.

The uses of the *moriche* palm (also called *ita*) are manifold. It is one of those all-purpose tropical plants, like agave. A Pemón Indian called Anita, whom we later travelled with, spoke of *las siete vidas de moriche* - its 'seven lives'. These are: *techo, ropa, hamaca, curiara, palmitos, gusano, cachire*. The first four are its practical uses: they use the leaves for roof-thatch, the fibres for weaving cloth and hammocks, and the wood for boat-building. The others are food sources. *Palmitos* are palm hearts, a great delicacy: the stem is carefully shaved with a machete till you get to the white heart, which looks something like a leek and has a crisp bland taste when raw. Ralegh observed this: 'they use the tops of *palmitos* for their bread'. The *gusano* is a grub that grows in the palm which they fatten for food. We saw some in a little tin in Benito's house: fat yellow maggots the size of a broad bean. These they eat fried, or crushed into a paste or butter, or sometimes just as they come: Delta crudities. *Cachire* is liquor, here a palm-wine: more often made from fermented manioc.

CHARLES NICHOLL, **The Creature in the Map.**

VEGETABLES AND SALAD

Ensalada Criolla
South American Salad

2 onions, finely sliced
Salt
1 hot green or red chilli, seeded and chopped
1.5 g/1/2 teaspoon dried oregano, crumbled
120ml/4 fl oz mild white vinegar
2 large tomatoes (225g/8 oz each) peeled
2 sweet red peppers, seeded and chopped
2 large cloves garlic, very finely sliced
15g/1 tablespoon finely chopped flat parsley
Salt, freshly ground pepper
Paprika, to taste
2.5 g/1/2 teaspoon dried oregano, crumbled
Vinaigrette to taste (3 parts oil to 1 part vinegar)

Put the sliced onions into a bowl with boiling water to cover. Add the salt, chilli, dried oregano and vinegar and leave for 1 hour. Remove the onion rings and discard the soaking liquid. Cut the tomatoes into 1cm/1/2 inch slices then into quarters. In a large salad bowl combine the onions, tomatoes, garlic, peppers, parsley, oregano, salt and pepper and paprika, if using, and toss gently to mix. Toss again with the dressing and serve to accompany grilled meats. *Serves 4-6.*

Calabacitas Picadas con Crema
Chopped Courgettes with Cream
MEXICO

2 tablespoons corn oil
450 g/1 lb tender young courgettes, coarsely chopped
1 onion, finely chopped
2 cloves garlic, chopped
1 or 2 small fresh green chillies, seeded and chopped
175 g/6 oz corn kernels, if frozen defrosted
1 tablespoon chopped fresh coriander
Salt, freshly ground pepper
225 ml/8 fl oz heavy cream, or sour cream

In a heavy saucepan or casserole heat the oil. Add the courgettes, onion, garlic and chillies and sauté, stirring over moderate heat for 3 or 4 minutes. Add the corn, coriander and salt and pepper to taste. Cover and cook over low heat until the courgettes are soft. Stir in the cream and cook long enough to heat through, but do not let it boil. If liked, use fresh jalapeño or poblano chillies. *Serves 4-6.*

Farofa
Toasted Cassava Meal
BRAZIL

Cassava or manioc originated in Brazil and is sprinkled on almost all savoury stews. It has a pleasantly nutty taste. Indian shops sell it as gari. As well as the everyday farofa there are many more elaborate versions with eggs, with raisins and olives, onions and with dendê (palm) oil.

50g/2 oz unsalted butter
225g/8 oz cassava meal
Salt

In a frying pan, over low heat, heat the butter and add the cassava meal. Cook, stirring, until the meal has absorbed the butter and is a light brown. Season with salt and serve at room temperature. *Serves 6.*

What he said so greatly impressed them that they were reassured, and more than two thousand of them came all together, and they all came to the Christians and placed their hands on their heads, which was a mark of great respect and friendship; yet they were all trembling until they had been greatly reassured. The Christians said that when at last they had lost their fear, they went to their houses, one and all, and each of them brought to them what they had to eat, which is bread of 'niamas' that is, of roots like large carrots which they grow, for they sow and grow and cultivate in all these lands, and it is their mainstay of life. They make bread from these roots and boil and roast them, and they taste like chestnuts, so that no one eating them would believe that they are anything but chestnuts. They gave them bread and fish, and whatever they had. And as the Indians whom he had in the ship had understood that the admiral wished to have a parrot, it seems that the Indian who went with the Christians told them something of this, and so they brought them parrots and gave them as many as they asked, without wishing to have anything in return.

The Journal of Christopher Columbus

Cazuela de Repollo
Cabbage with Sauce
BOLIVIA

1 white or green cabbage weighing 900g/2 lbs
Salt
30ml/2 tablespoons olive oil
2 onions, finely chopped
1 sweet red pepper, seeded and chopped

3 cloves garlic, chopped
115g/4 oz bacon, rind removed and chopped
1 or more small fresh red chillies seeded and chopped (optional)
675g/1 1/2 lbs tomatoes, peeled, seeded and chopped
Salt, freshly ground pepper
120ml/4 fl oz dry white wine
6 small freshly cooked new potatoes, peeled

Wash and core the cabbage and shred it. Put it into a large saucepan of briskly boiling salted water, bring back to a boil over high heat and cook, uncovered, for 5 minutes. Drain, set aside, reserve the cooking liquid.

In a frying pan heat the olive oil, add the onions, pepper, garlic, bacon and chillies, if using, and sauté until the vegetables are tender. Add the tomatoes and cook, stirring from time to time, until the mixture is well blended. Transfer the cabbage to a casserole, stir in the vegetable-tomato mixture and season to taste with salt and pepper. Add the wine and the potatoes, cover and cook for 5 minutes until the cabbage is heated through. If the casserole is at all dry, add a little of the reserved cabbage water. It should be moist but not runny. *Serves 6.*

F or supper each wife chooses a choice piece from her share and sets it to simmer in a pot of manioc or taro. Each in turn comes to deposit at our feet a helping of the stew served on tachau, large earthenware plates with a black glaze. Wajari has been similarly served and summons his two adolescent sons, Chiwian and Paantam, to share his meal, while Senur, Entza and Mirunik gather their respective children around them for a little family feast. Although the wives sometimes eat together, each usually prepares the food for herself and her own children. Even within the family group such occasional commensality does not lead to shared dishes. The Achuar have clearly never heard of primitive communism.

A gourd of water is passed round as a ewer, for the pre-meal ablutions: a gulp to rinse one's mouth, then a gulp ejected in a thin stream, to wash one's hands. The master of the house then invites me to begin with the stereotyped injunction, 'Eat the manioc!' to which one has to respond with embarrassed acquiescence and a show of surprise at suddenly discovering the steaming dishes at one's feet. Sweet manioc is the staple food of the Achuar, as synonymous with nourishment as bread is in France and, even when taken as an accompaniment to a dish of choice game, it is always this modest root that one is deprecatingly invited to eat. It is good form for the guest to continue for a while to ignore this invitation, as if already well-satisfied and incapable of swallowing a single mouthful. Only under the duress of the laws of politeness does one finally force oneself to peck at the dishes until then painstakingly ignored.

Philippe Descola, **The Spears of Twilight: Life and Death in the Amazon Jungle**

Kiveve
Mashed West Indian Pumpkin
PARAGUAY

The preferred vegetable for this is sold in Caribbean markets as West Indian pumpkin, or *calabaza* where Spanish is spoken.

450 g/1 lb West Indian pumpkin, peeled and cut into chunks
Salt
50 g/2 oz yellow maize meal
4 tablespoons butter
2 teaspoons light brown sugar (optional)
450 g/1 lb Ricotta cheese
350 ml/12 fl oz water
2 tablespoons butter

Put the pumpkin chunks in a saucepan with enough salted water to cover, bring to a simmer, cover and cook until tender. Drain, set aside and keep warm. Pour the water into a heavy saucepan and bring to a boil. Pour in the maize meal in a slow, steady stream stirring constantly with a wooden spoon. Continue to cook, over low heat, stirring constantly, until the maize meal is thick enough to hold its shape. Off the heat, add the pumpkin, butter, and salt and pepper to taste. Mix well then mix in the Ricotta cheese. Return the mixture to the heat and cook, stirring, until it is heated through. Serve hot with grilled and roast meat or poultry. *Serves 6.*

Ensalada de Cebolla con Tomates
Onion and Tomato Salad
CHILE

Salt
1 large onion, thinly sliced
450 g/1 lb tomatoes, peeled and chopped
2 sweet green peppers, seeded and finely chopped
1 clove garlic, finely chopped (optional)
Salt, pepper
Vinaigrette

Mix the salt with enough cold water to cover the onion, and soak the onion for 15 minutes. Drain and pat dry. In a salad bowl combine all the ingredients, season with salt and pepper and the garlic if using, and toss to mix.

Dress with the vinaigrette, 3 tablespoons olive oil and 1 tablespoon mild vinegar or to taste. *Serves 4-6.*

Cuajado de Verduras
Mixed Vegetables with Eggs
COLOMBIA

100 g/4 oz cooked carrots, cut in 1.2 cm/1/2 inch pieces
100 g/4 oz cooked green peas
100 g/4 oz cooked calabaza (West Indian pumpkin) cut into pieces
6 spring onions trimmed and coarsely chopped, using white and green parts
3 tablespoons butter
2 medium onions, finely chopped
450 g/1 lb tomatoes, peeled, seeded and chopped
Salt and freshly ground pepper
4 large eggs

In a bowl combine the cooked vegetables, and the spring onions. Set aside. In a frying pan heat the butter and sauté the onions until they are soft but not brown. Add the tomatoes and cook until the mixture is slightly thickened. Add the reserved vegetables, stir to mix, and season with salt and pepper. In a bowl beat the eggs lightly and pour over the vegetable mixture. Cook over moderate heat until the eggs have set. Eat as a light luncheon or supper dish. *Serves 4-6.*

Ensalada de Papaya
Pawpaw salad
BOLIVIA

Slice cucumbers thinly crossways mix with an equal amount of ripe pawpaw cut into cubes and toss in an oil, salt and lemon juice dressing.

Yuca con Ajo
Cassava with Garlic Sauce
CUBA

> 450 g/1 lb cassava (yucca) root
> Salt
> 4 large cloves garlic, finely chopped
> 3 tablespoons olive oil
> 1 tablespoon light vinegar

Peel the cassava root under cold running water as it discolours quickly. Cut it into 1.2 cm/1/2 inch slices and boil in salted water until tender about 30 minutes. The vegetable may break up in cooking but this does not matter. Drain and pat dry with paper towels. Mix together the garlic, olive oil and vinegar and pour over the cassava, tossing to mix. Serve as an appetizer or salad.

B reakfast is generally nonexistent or else a piece of toast with butter and *café con leche* (coffee with milk). Cubans rarely eat eggs in the morning; a 5,000-family survey by the Cuban Consumer Institute found that only 1 percent of the households ate eggs for breakfast. Nor do they drink fruit juice, which is difficult to obtain.

Midmorning and afternoon snacks are usually sweet: a piece of cake or pie, yogurt with plenty of sugar, soda, or an ice cream cone. Or it might be a buttered roll with a croquette, a fried meat patty, an omelette, or sometimes a sandwich of just plain mayonnaise.

Lunch and dinner differ little one from another. Most common is a plate of black beans or split peas, rice, some kind of meat, chicken, fish or eggs, *vianda* (if available), and bread. The most common desserts are cream cheese with guava jam, custard, bread pudding, and rice pudding.

The menu for festive occasions - whether at the workplace, neighborhood committee, birthday or wedding - is standard: *congri* or *moros y cristianos* (beans and rice cooked together), pork, yucca, tomato salad (optional), bread, cake, soda, and beer.

The old saying 'sin arroz no hay comida' (without rice, it's not a meal) still holds true for the majority of Cubans. When rice quotas were cut in 1966, Cubans went to the extreme of cutting spaghetti into tiny pieces to resemble rice. The rice tradition came to Cuba from Africa (through the slave trade), Spain (through the colonizers), and China (through the contracted workers).

The U.S. embargo, a sharp decline in rice production in the first years of the revolution, and the cutoff of rice imports from China in the late 1960s made wheat more important. Spaghetti and macaroni made from imported wheat have become staples in the Cuban diet since the revolution. And bread and crackers, previously identified with wealthy urban diets, are now daily fare for everyone.

MEDEA BENJAMIN, JOSEPH COLLINS and MICHAEL SCOTT, **No Free Lunch: Food and Revolution in Cuba Today**

Buñuelos de Espinaca
Spinach Fritters
ARGENTINA

2 tablespoons olive oil
175 g/6 oz spinach, finely chopped
100 g/4 oz tomatoes, peeled, seeded and chopped
1 onion, finely chopped
1 clove garlic, chopped
1/2 medium green or red pepper, seeded and finely chopped
1 or more small fresh green or red chillies, seeded and finely chopped
Salt, freshly ground pepper
1 tablespoon freshly grated Parmesan
100 g/4 oz plain flour
1 teaspoon baking powder
1 large egg, well beaten
125 ml/4 fl oz milk, about
Peanut or corn oil for frying

Heat the oil in a large, heavy frying pan and add the spinach, tomatoes, onion garlic, pepper and chillies. Stir to mix and sauté over moderate heat, stirring from time to time until all the vegetables are soft. Off the heat, season with salt and pepper and stir in the Parmesan. Set aside. In a bowl sift together the flour and baking powder. Stir in the egg mixed with half the milk adding more milk if necessary to make a smooth mixture. Add more as needed. Stir in the vegetable mixture, mixing well. Wipe out the frying pan, pour in some oil and heat. Drop in the mixture by the teaspoon. Fry until golden brown all over. Drain on paper towels and serve hot. Makes about 20 fritters.

Ensalada de Naranjas
Orange Salad
GUATEMALA

There are innumerable orange salads, yet Guatemala has managed to invent a new one. It is widely popular. Salt brings out the flavour of the oranges which might well explain the popularity of the fruit in salads with salty dressings.

6 oranges
45g/3 tablespoons pepitas (pumpkin seeds)
Serrano chillies, seeded and very finely chopped, or dried red chillies, crumbled, to taste.
Salt

Peel the oranges, remove all the white pith then cut into crossways slices about 1 cm/1/2 inch thick. Refrigerate while preparing the pumpkin seeds. In a dry frying pan over moderate heat, toast the pumpkin seeds until they are lightly browned. Cool and grind finely in a nut grinder or small coffee mill. Shake through a sieve into a bowl. Have the chillies ready chopped in another small bowl.

Arrange the oranges on individual plates, sprinkle with salt, then pumpkin seeds and top with chilli to taste. *Serves 6.*

Among the Chonos Islands, a wild potato grows in abundance, which in general habit is even more closely similar to the cultivated kind than is the *maglia* of Molina.

These potatoes grow near the sea-beach, in thick beds, on a sandy, shelly soil wherever the trees are not too close together. In the middle of January they were in flower, but the tubers were small, and few in number; especially in those plants which grew in the shade, and had the most luxuriant foliage. Nevertheless, I found one which was of an oval form, with one diameter two inches in length. The raw bulbs had precisely the smell of the common potato of England, but when cooked they shrunk, and became watery and insipid. They had not a bitter taste, as, according to Molina, is the case with the Chilian kind; and they could be eaten with safety. Some plants measured from the ground to the tip of the upper leaf, not less than four feet.

So very close is the general resemblance with the cultivated species, that it is necessary to show that they have not been imported. The simple fact of their growth on the islands, and even small rocks, throughout the Chonos Archipelago, which has never been inhabited, and very seldom visited, is an argument of some weight. But the circumstance of the wildest Indian tribes being well acquainted with the plant, is stronger. Mr. Lowe, a very intelligent and active sealer, informs me that on showing some potatoes to the naked savages in the Gulf of Trinidad (lat. 50°), they immediately recognised them, and calling them 'Aquina,' wanted to take them away. The savages also pointed to a place where they grew; which fact was subsequently verified. The Indians of Chiloé, belonging to another tribe, also give them a name in their own language. The simple fact of their being known and named by distinct races, over a space of four or five hundred miles on a most unfrequented and scarcely known coast, almost proves their native existence. Professor Henslow, who has examined the dried specimens which I brought home, says that they are the same as those described by Mr. Sabine from Valparaíso, but that they form a variety which by some botanists has been considered as specifically distinct. It is remarkable that the same plant should be found on the sterile mountains of central Chile, where a drop of rain does not fall more than six months, and within the damp forests of the southern islands. From what we know of the habits of the potato, this latter situation would appear more congenial than the former, as its birthplace.

CHARLES DARWIN, **Voyage of HMS Beagle, 1831 - 1836: Journal of Researches**

Ocopa Arequipeña
Potatoes with Walnut, Cheese and Chilli sauce
PERU

> 125 ml/4 fl oz corn or peanut oil
> 1 medium onion cut into very thick slices
> 2 cloves garlic, chopped
> 4-6 small fresh hot red chillies, seeded and chopped
> 100 g/4 oz broken walnut meats
> 100 g/4 oz curd or Ricotta cheese
> 225 ml/8 fl oz whole milk
> Salt
> Lettuce leaves
> 900 g/2 lbs medium sized potatoes, or 6 of uniform size
> 6 hard-boiled eggs, halved lengthways
> 12 pitted black olives
> Strips of red pepper, preferably pimiento, for garnish

In a small heavy saucepan heat the oil, add the onion and garlic and cook over very low heat until the onion slices are golden. Transfer the oil, onion, garlic, chillies, walnut meats and cheese to a food processor. Pour in the milk, season with salt to taste and process to a smooth sauce, the consistency of a heavy mayonnaise. Meanwhile cook, peel and halve the potatoes lengthways. Have ready a large, warmed oval platter. Line the platter with lettuce leaves and arrange the potatoes cut side down on top of the lettuce. Mask the potatoes with the sauce. Arrange the eggs, cut side up, among the potatoes in a decorative pattern. Garnish with the black olives and red pepper strips. Serve as a first course, or the main course for a light luncheon or supper. *Serves 6.*

Ensalada de Verduras
Mixed Vegetable Platter
ECUADOR

> Vinaigrette
> Cooked green beans cut into 1.2 cm/1/2 inch pieces
> Cooked beetroot, diced
> Cooked cauliflower, separated into florets
> Cooked courgettes, diced
> Cooked carrots, diced
> Cooked potatoes, diced
> Cooked corn kernels
> Diced celery
> Sliced tomatoes

Make the vinaigrette using 3 tablespoons of olive oil to 1 tablespoon of mild vinegar. Season with salt and pepper. Choose a large platter, preferably oval. The choice of vegetables is flexible; the ones listed are the ones most used but asparagus, quartered artichoke hearts, green peas and sliced avocado are also popular. Vegetables should be cooked separately, drained and lightly seasoned with the vinaigrette. They are served at room temperature as are the fresh vegetables. Arrange the vegetables in rows at each end of the platter choosing colours that are attractive, carrots a bright orange, next to white potatoes for example. In the centre of the platter have a heap of sliced tomatoes. Choose very ripe well flavoured ones. Serve to accompany a main course. It is also an attractive dish for a buffet. Garnish, if liked, with sliced hard-boiled egg and black and green olives.

Caviar Criollo
Mashed Black Beans
VENEZUELA

> 225 g/8 oz black haricot beans
> 2 tablespoons olive oil
> 1 onion, finely chopped
> 1 red pepper, seeded and finely chopped
> 3 cloves garlic, chopped
> 1/4 teaspoon ground cumin
> Salt

Wash and pick over the beans and soak in cold water for about 4 hours. Put into a heavy saucepan with water to cover by 2.5 cm/1 inch, bring to a boil, lower the heat to a simmer, cover and cook until the beans are tender, about 2 hours. The time will vary according to the age of the beans, so check from time to time and add more water if necessary. Set the cooked beans aside. In a frying pan heat the oil and sauté the onion and pepper until they are soft. Add the garlic and cumin and cook for a minute or so longer, then stir the mixture into the beans. Salt to taste and cook, partially covered for half an hour longer when the beans should be quite dry. Mash the beans to a smooth paste adding a little more olive oil, if liked. Serve as an appetizer.

Ode to an Onion

Onion,
luminous flask,
petal by petal
was your beauty fashioned,
crystalline scales your girth increased
and, hidden in the dark earth,
your belly swelled with dew.
Beneath the ground
occurred the miracle
and when your awkward, callow shoot
first peered,
and when, like swords
your first leaves pierced the plot,
earth assembled all her might,
displaying your translucent nudity.
And, as the alien sea,
in swelling the breasts of Aphrodite
repeated the magnolia,
so did the earth
create you,
onion,
pellucid planet
destined to glow,
constant constellation,
spherical water rose,

upon
the table
of the poor.
Magnanimous,
you undo your bulb of freshness
in the hot consummation
of the cooking pot;
and the crystal shred
in the burning heat of oil
becomes a feathery golden ring.
Then, too, I shall record as useful
your influence on the love of salad,
and even Heaven, it seems,
in giving you the delicate form of hail,
proclaims your chopped transparency
on the tomato's hemispheres.
But, within the reach
of common folk,
oil-moistened
and sprinkled
with a bit of salt,
you stave off the hunger
of the labourer along his toilsome way.
Star of the poor,
fairy godmother,

enveloped
in delicate paper,
you emerge from earth
eternal, integral, a pure
celestial offshoot.
And at the chop
of the kitchen knife,
there wells up
the only tear we shed
without woe.
Without afflicting us you made us weep.
All that is, onion, I have sung,
but to me, you are
lovelier than a bird
of dazzling plumage;
you are, to me,
heavenly sphere, platinum goblet,
motionless dance
of the snowy anemone.

And in your crystalline nature
resides the fragrance of the earth.

PABLO NERUDA, **Elemental Odes**

SAUCES

SAUCES

Sauces are integral to a large proportion of Latin America's dishes. Meat, poultry or seafood is either cooked in a sauce to absorb the flavours or steeped in the sauce at the end of the cooking process. Traditionally, they are quite unlike European sauces as the pre-conquest Americas had no cream, butter, hen's eggs or wheat flour on which many of our own sauces are based. Peppers and tomatoes are the key ingredients in most Latin American sauces, though it is hard to generalise about such a diverse aspect of cooking. The Spanish word for sauce, *salsa*, tends to be applied to hot chilli sauces. All over Latin America, hot chilli salsas appear on meal tables to be added to dishes at will. Hot salsas are also popular outside Latin America. In the South West of the USA, salsa is the name given to a sauce made from onions, hot chilli peppers, tomatoes, and lemon juice or red wine vinegar. More recently, commercially produced salsa has appeared on our supermarket shelves as a relish or dip for tortilla chips.

Caribbean sauces have one thing in common: they are hot, chilli pepper hot. But aside from their heat, they vary enormously. Trinidad adds curry powder and turmeric, Dominica grates raw green papaya, and Martinique uses fresh lime juice to give its hot sauce a special flavour. The hottest chilli sauce I ever had was in Yucatán, called *Ixni-Pec*, pronounced roughly schnee-peck. The Yucatáns say they have an even hotter one made with just *habañero* chillies. As well as being hot, the habañero pepper has an exquisite flavour, once tasted never forgotten. In Guatemala, in honour of its ferocity, it is known as *chile caballero*, the gentleman chilli. Some foolhardy souls think it is manly or *macho* to eat very hot peppers. I was once present at a dinner when a photographer friend of mine was boasting about his ability to eat pickled *jalapeño* chillies straight out of his hand. Alas he forgot the golden rule when dealing with chillies which is to wash your hands in warm soapy water after handling them. He inadvertently rubbed his eye with his hand and let out a mighty yelp.

A basic sauce, really a cooking base, is called *sofrito* and originally came to the Americas from Spain. Sofrito means lightly fried and the Spanish version consisted of onions, garlic, ham, sausage, herbs, salt and black peppercorns fried in olive oil. In Latin America, tomatoes and peppers were added and in some Caribbean islands, Puerto Rico and Cuba for example, annato (achiote) is used to colour and flavour the oil. This is made from the hard orange-red pulp seeds of a small flowering tree of tropical America, *Bixa orellana*. The seeds give off a rich orange-red colour when cooked, and colour oil when briefly heated in it. They also have considerable flavour.

In Puerto Rico the sofrito starts with a mixture called *recado básico*. The name comes from the Spanish *recado*, the day's shopping. It is made of onions, sweet peppers, garlic and leaves of *recao* pureed in a blender, bottled and refrigerated for immediate use and frozen if made in large batches. *Recao* is a broad-leafed coriander, *Ergynium foetidum*, a stronger, bolder relative of the European coriander, *Coriandum sativum*. If it is not available, just use fresh coriander. This is mixed with the fried onions, garlic, ham, sausage and tomatoes of the original sofrito. It can be the starting point for numerous soups, stews and marinades. Slightly changed, it makes a good dip. The sofrito can be thickened with ground almonds, sieved hard-boiled egg yolks or bread crumbs. In Cuba, sofritos are sold commercially and will keep much longer than the home-made version. Like the Puerto Rican version, Cuban sofrito is made with annatto.

Another sauce, *adobo*, is almost as much a cooking method (*adobada*) as a sauce and is found throughout the region. Made of vinegar, chillies and salt, it was originally used to preserve meats, a pickling sauce. Herbs, spices and garlic add flavour and variety to the region's adobos.

Once mangoes had been introduced to the Americas, they were used in sauces too, especially on the Caribbean islands. Martinique and Guadeloupe have a green mango relish (*rougail de mangues vertes*) that makes a delicious first course by itself and is good with fish and cold meats, as well as with curry. It clearly derives from an Indian original, probably adapted from the indentured workers who came to the French islands. Latin American and Caribbean cooks are clever at using ingredients to mimic unavailable ones : lacking apples, an 'apple sauce' is made using green (unripe) papayas (pawpaws) and a tart, cherry sauce is made using *acerolas*, Barbados cherries, and served with chicken, duck or pork, or with cooked green vegetables.

Peanuts, indigenous to South America, are used in sauces in a variety of ways. Peru, for example, is credited with inventing peanut butter. I am particularly fond of a peanut sauce from Ecuador. Many Latin American sauces are thickened with nuts, a colonial inheritance from Spain with Middle Eastern overtones.

The avocado, *Persea americana*, of the laurel family was cultivated in Mexico as far back as 7000 BC. Its name in Nahuatl, the langugage of the Aztecs, was *ahuacatl*, not so very far removed from the name we use today in English-speaking countries, which derives from *aguacate*, the Spanish version of the Ancient Mexican. In Aztec Mexico, avocados were used to make the salad/sauce *guacamole*, still popular today. Over the centuries the avocado spread throughout the region and acquired new names in the process. In the Andean countries, it is known by its Quechua name of *palta*, though in some parts of South America it keeps its Mexican name. In Brazil it is called *abacate*.

A cut avocado discolours quickly when it is exposed to the air. To keep a halved avocado, leave the stone in place, brush the cut surfaces with lemon juice, cover with cling film, then refrigerate. I have found the best way to mash an avocado is to halve it, discard the stone, mash it in its shell with a fork, holding the shell in the palm of the hand. The mashed flesh can now be scooped out easily without the fruit slithering around the bowl. It is better not to process the flesh in a food processor or blender, as it should retain some texture.

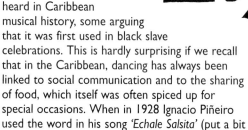

When New York's Fania record company wanted to raise the profile of their salsa musicians in the early 1970s, they needed a simple, effective term which would enable people to instantly identify their product. The word chosen was salsa. In fact, the word has often been heard in Caribbean musical history, some arguing that it was first used in black slave celebrations. This is hardly surprising if we recall that in the Caribbean, dancing has always been linked to social communication and to the sharing of food, which itself was often spiced up for special occasions. When in 1928 Ignacio Piñeiro used the word in his song *'Echale Salsita'* (put a bit of sauce in it), he was using the term to imply the pleasure produced by hearing a number of instruments played and combined harmoniously. An exciting, exotic 'instrumental sauce' that could help digest the hardships of daily routine.

> One night I left home in search of adventure
> looking for a taste of pleasure and fun
> oh my God what a time I had
> I spent the night in a whirl,
> left behind the lights of home
> and found myself in a real party.
>
> In Catalina I found something unexpected
> a voice that cried out like this:
> 'put a little sauce in it,
> put a little sauce in it!'
> *Echale Salsita,* version by Ignacio Piñeiro

HERNANDO CALVO OSPINA, **Salsa: Havana Heat, Bronx Beat**

SAUCES

Salsa Cruda
Fresh Tomato Sauce
Mexico

Freshly made, this sauce is on the table at every meal in Mexico, eaten with fish, shellfish, poultry and meats as well as with tacos, etc. Makes about two and a half 225g/8 oz cups

> 450 g/ 1 lb red ripe tomatoes, peeled and finely chopped
> 2 or more small hot fresh green chillies seeded and chopped, or use canned serrano chillies, seeded and chopped
> 1 tablespoon fresh coriander, chopped
> Salt

In a bowl combine all the ingredients as soon as possible before serving. Toss to mix and serve in the bowl at room temperature.

Salsa Verde
Green Tomato Sauce
Mexico

Mexican green (husk) tomatoes (tomatillos) are seldom available in our markets. If you cannot find them use tinned ones. The sauce is as popular as Salsa Cruda and appears on tables daily. Makes about 350 g/12 oz

> 225g/8 oz fresh tomatillos, husked and rinsed or 275g/10 oz tin, drained
> 1 tablespoon finely chopped onion
> 1 or more fresh small hot green chillies, seeded and chopped
> 1 tablespoon fresh coriander, chopped
> Salt

If using fresh green tomatoes simmer them in salted water for 3 or 4 minutes until tender. Drain and cool. In a food processor combine the tomatoes, onion, chillies and coriander and process briefly to a coarse purée. Pour into a bowl and let stand about 30 minutes before serving.

Sauce Ti-Malice
Chilli Sauce
Haiti

> 1 large onion (about 225g/8 oz) finely chopped
> 2 cloves garlic, finely chopped
> 2 spring onions, finely chopped (white part only)
> 3 tablespoons lime juice
> 2 small fresh chillies, preferably red, seeded and chopped
> Salt, freshly ground pepper
> 2 tablespoons olive oil

In a bowl combine the onion, garlic and spring onions with the lime juice and stand in a cool place for about an hour. Transfer to a small saucepan with all the remaining ingredients except the olive oil and bring to a boil over moderate heat. Stir and remove from the heat. Cool and stir in the oil. Chill slightly if liked and serve with meat dishes. It is especially good with pork.

Salsa de Maní
Peanut Sauce
Ecuador

> 2 tablespoons annatto (achiote) oil, (see below)
> 1 medium onion, finely chopped
> 2 cloves garlic, chopped
> 1 large tomato (225 g/ 8 oz), or 2 medium, peeled, seeded and chopped
> 4 tablespoons smooth peanut butter
> Salt

In a frying pan heat the annatto oil. Add the onion and cook over moderate heat until it is tender. Add the garlic and sauté for a few minutes longer then stir in the tomato and cook until the mixture is well blended, about 10 minutes. Stir in the peanut butter mixing well, season with salt and cook just long enough to heat through. If the sauce is very thick, thin it with tomato juice to pouring consistency and heat through.

In Ecuador the sauce is served with potato cakes. It is also good with fried fish, chicken, and vegetables, especially cooked cabbage.

Annatto (Achiote) Oil
> 3 tablespoons annatto seeds (achiote)
> 3 tablespoons peanut (groundnut) or similar oil

In a small heavy saucepan combine the annatto and the oil over moderate heat and cook until the seeds begin to give up their colour, a deep orange red. This will happen in about 1 minute if the seeds are fresh. Do not heat any longer once the colour begins to turn to golden. Remove from the heat immediately, cool, strain and bottle. Refrigerated the oil will keep indefinitely. Use to colour and flavour foods.

Salsa de Perejil
Parsley Sauce
Chile

> 50g/2 oz parsley, preferably flat-leaved continental parsley, very finely chopped
> 225ml/8 fl oz olive oil, or vegetable oil such as peanut
> 4 tablespoons white vinegar or lemon juice
> 1/2 teaspoon Dijon mustard
> Salt, freshly ground pepper

In a bowl whisk all the ingredients together combining into a vinaigrette-like sauce. Chill slightly and serve with fish and shellfish or as a dressing for tomato salad.

Salsa, an early Californian sauce

> 450g/1 lb tomatoes, peeled and finely chopped
> 1 medium red onion, chopped
> 1 sweet red or green pepper, seeded and finely chopped
> 1 small hot chilli, preferably red, seeded and finely chopped
> 1 tablespoon lemon juice
> Salt, freshly ground pepper

Combine all the ingredients in a bowl, stirring to mix well. Chill thoroughly and serve with fish or steaks.

Begin shelling the nuts several days in advance, for that is a big job to which many hours must be devoted. After the shell is removed, you still have to take off the skin that covers the nut. Take care that none of this skin, not a single bit, is left clinging to the nuts, because when they're ground and mixed with the cream, any skin will make the nut sauce bitter, and all of your previous work will have been for nothing.

Tita and Chencha were finishing shelling the nuts, sitting around the kitchen table. The nuts were to be used for the chillies in nut sauce they would be serving as the main course at the next day's wedding. All the other members of the family had gone, deserting the kitchen table on one pretext or another. Only these two indefatigable women were continuing at the bottom of the mountain. To tell the truth, Tita didn't blame the others. They had given her enough help already that week; she knew quite well that it wasn't easy to shell a thousand nuts without getting sick of it. The only person she knew who could do it without any sign of fatigue was Mama Elena.

Not only could she crack sack after sack of nuts in a short time, she seemed to take great pleasure in doing it.

Applying pressure, smashing to bits, skinning, those were among her favourite activities. The hours just flew by when she sat on the patio with a sack of nuts between her legs, not getting up until she was done with it.

For her it would have been child's play to crack those thousand nuts, which required so much effort from everyone else. They needed that enormous quantity because for each twenty-five chillies they had to shell one hundred nuts; so it figured that for two hundred and fifty chillies, they needed a thousand nuts.

LAURA ESQUIVEL, **Like Water for Chocolate**

Salsa Fresca
Fresh Sauce

Popular in the southwest of the USA with hamburgers and as a dipping sauce.

> 275g/10 oz tomatoes, peeled, seeded and chopped
> 125g/4 oz onion, finely chopped
> 125g/4 oz sweet green peppers, seeded and finely chopped
> 1 clove garlic, chopped or more to taste
> Salt

Combine all the ingredients, except the salt, in a bowl. Season to taste with salt and toss to mix thoroughly. Let stand for no longer than 30 minutes and serve at room temperature. The sauce does not keep and should be used the day it is made.

Vatapá
BRAZIL

This is a good example of the Latin American method of cooking food in a sauce which is an integral part of the dish. Usually made with chicken or prawns and fish, it is one of the truly great dishes of the Bahian kitchen of Brazil and has local, African and Portuguese influences.

> 2 tablespoons olive oil
> 2 medium onions, finely chopped
> 2 cloves garlic, chopped
> 450 g/1 lb tomatoes, chopped
> 2 small chillies, seeded and chopped
> Salt
> 2 tablespoons lime or lemon juice
> 4 tablespoons fresh coriander, coarsely chopped
> 2 1.1 kg/2 1/2lb chickens, quartered, or 700g/1 1/2lb raw prawns, shelled and deveined and 700g/1 1/2 lb fillets any firm white fish such as cod cut into 5 cm/2-inch pieces
> 225g/8 oz finely ground almonds, cashews or peanuts
> 225g/8 oz dried shrimps, finely ground
> 700 ml/1 1/4 pt thin coconut milk
> 225 ml/8 fl oz thick coconut milk
> 1 tablespoon rice flour
> 4 tablespoons dendê (palm) oil

In a heavy saucepan, or large frying pan that has a lid heat the oil and sauté the onions, garlic, tomatoes and chillies for 5 minutes until tender. Season the mixture with salt. Stir in the lime or lemon juice and the coriander. Add the chickens, or prawns and fish whichever is being used, and simmer, over low heat, covered for about 35 minutes for the chickens or until they are tender, and about 10 minutes for the fish. Cook the prawns only until they turn pink and have lost their translucent look, about 3 minutes. If using chickens, lift them out, skin and bone them and chop coarsely. Lift out the fish and prawns and set them aside.

Put the vegetable mixture through a sieve, pressing down hard on the solids to extract all the flavour. Return the liquid to the saucepan and add the nuts, dried shrimps, and the thin coconut milk. Simmer for 15 minutes. Add the thick coconut milk and the rice flour mixed with a little water, stir and cook uncovered until the mixture has the consistency of a thick béchamel. Add the poultry, prawns and fish, whichever is being used, and the dendê oil and cook just long enough to heat through. *Serves 6 to 8 generously.*

NOTE: For those disinclined to make their own coconut milk, creamed coconut gives excellent results. Simply dilute with water to the desired consistency, thin coconut milk like milk, thick coconut milk like double cream.

P asa is what the Indians of Peru call a certain clay, which is white with a few brown spots like soap... it is used by them as a highly prized sauce, with which, dissolved and with salt, they eat their *papas* and other roots, moistening them in this mud as if it were mustard, and for this reason it is sold in the plazas of all the towns.

Sophie D. Coe, **Lobo 1880-1893** quoted in **America's First Cuisines**

Salsa de Naranjas
Orange Sauce
Widely popular in the region as a dessert sauce

100g/4 oz granulated sugar
1 tablespoon cornflour
350ml/12 fl oz freshly squeezed, strained orange juice
1 tablespoon lemon juice
2 tablespoons unsalted butter, cut in bits

In a bowl mix together the sugar and cornflour then stir in the orange and lemon juices blending until smooth. Transfer to a saucepan and cook over very low heat, stirring constantly, until the butter has been absorbed. Serve warm as a topping for cakes or puddings.

Pawpaw (papaya) Sauce
Jamaica and English-speaking islands

900g/2 lbs green (unripe) pawpaw peeled, seeded and chopped coarsely
1/4 teaspoon ground allspice

1/4 teaspoon salt
225ml/8 fl oz water
Light brown sugar to taste
4 tablespoons lime juice

In a large heavy saucepan combine the pawpaw, allspice, salt and water and bring to a boil over moderate heat. Reduce the heat to low, cover and simmer, stirring from time to time, until mixture is soft. The water should have been absorbed; if not, cook, uncovered, for a little longer. Cool slightly and reduce to a purée in a food processor. Return the purée to the saucepan and stir in the sugar to taste and the lime juice. Cook, stirring until the sugar has dissolved and the mixture has the consistency of apple sauce. When cool, transfer to a container and refrigerate until ready to use. Use instead of apple sauce. Makes about 475g/1 lb.

Guacamole
Avocado Sauce
Mexico

Guacamole is probably the oldest of Mexico's sauces, evolved from an Aztec original. It has become a favourite the world over with every cuisine adding its own touches. It seems a shame not to give a classic Mexican version.

2 large avocados, pitted and mashed with a fork
1 medium tomato, peeled and chopped
1/2 small white onion, finely chopped
1 or more small fresh hot chillies, or to taste, seeded and chopped
1 tablespoon fresh coriander, chopped
Salt

In a bowl mix all the ingredients together and, if liked, place one of the avocado pits in the centre. This is supposed to keep the guacamole from darkening. The better plan is to make it just before serving but if it is made ahead of time, cover it with cling film and refrigerate it. If it darkens, stir in the dark part as it does no harm.

DESSERTS

DESSERTS

FRUITS FOR AN EMPEROR

Up until the Spanish conquest, Latin America had no dairy cattle, and hence no milk, cream or butter. Since there was no wheat, there was no flour for bread or pastries. Nor was there any cane sugar or domestic hens. The indigenous people of the Americas ate quail, duck, and dove eggs but these were not the same as those used in European desserts. What the region did have was an abundance of fruit. The Emperor Moctezuma is believed to have enjoyed *tamales* stuffed with strawberries which were sweetened with honey and flavoured with vanilla, another Mexican gift to the world's larder.

Among the strange fruits encountered by Spanish colonists was the *chirimoya* described by fruit expert Elizabeth Schneider as a jade-coloured fruit shaped like a pine cone. The chirimoya is a member of the *annonas* fruit family, the name coming from Quechua, a language still spoken by Indian communities in the Andes where the fruit originated. The subtle taste of the creamy chirimoya is reminiscent of mango, papaya, pineapple and vanilla. It was my mother's favourite American fruit. As well as annonas, the Spanish conquerors found custard apples (*A. reticulata*), soursops and sweetsops (*A. squamosa*). Soursop (Mexican *guanabana*) looks like cotton wool stuffed full of black seeds. Despite its texture, it yields a juice that makes an exquisite soft drink.

Then there are *zapotes*, native to the Mexican highlands and Central America and a favourite fruit in the Caribbean islands. Best known of these is the *chico zapote*, from the tree used to make 'chicle' or chewing gum. It has a brown skin and soft beige-coloured flesh. I have heard it called *sapodilla*, naseberry or simply *chico*. There are other members of the *zapote* group, one with black flesh, another with white. Then there is the star apple which shows a star pattern when halved. In Jamaica it is scooped out and mixed with orange juice to make a drink called 'matrimony'. *Guava*, native to Brazil, were another fruit that was new to the conquerors. Guava have a wonderful aroma and are used to make guava paste (sometimes known as guava cheese), one of the most popular regional desserts, especially in Mexico. The paste is served with cream cheese and can be bought ready made. Guava are also cooked in syrup and canned or made into jam and jelly. These were all colonial creations, made possible with the arrival of sugar.

In Uruguay and Paraguay the Spaniards stumbled across the *fejoa*, an egg-shaped fruit sometimes known as a 'pineapple guava'. Like guava, they have a wonderful perfume. In fact, both are members of the myrtle family which produces various aromatics such as allspice and cloves. Another unique fruit is the Peruvian *tamarillo*, or tree tomato, whose fruit can be scarlet or yellow. Then there are all those fruits which can now be bought off the shelf in our supermarkets but which were an astonishment to the Spanish and Portuguese: passion fruit, pineapple, *papaya* (pawpaw), tuna, fruit of the *nopal* (prickly pear) cactus and the far less known *pithaya*, fruit of the organ cactus. There may have been coconuts, and almost certainly there were plantains, a close relative of the sweet banana. Unlike bananas, plantains must be cooked before they can be eaten and come in three forms: green, semi-ripe and ripe (bananas were introduced at a later date). To this wealth of fruit the Spaniards added apples, plums, apricots, cherries, mangoes, pomegranates, melons, oranges, limes, lemons and grapes, giving Latin Americans fruits from all over the world.

A MIX OF BOTH WORLDS

The introduction of gelatine to South American cooks opened up all sorts of possibilities when combined with the revolutionary culinary changes the conquest had already brought about. The colonial ladies of the house, the *señoras*, left the basic cooking of soups, stews and vegetables to their cooks while they concentrated on the sweet things: puddings, jellies, cakes and biscuits. They were magnificently creative. A simple mix of orange juice sharpened with a little lime juice, some eggs and gelatine creates an attractively flavoured dessert enmoulded onto a decorative platter and served with whipped cream. Flavoured jellies became extremely popular and still are. Any fruit can be used and often the jellies are made with milk. Gelatine and cream mixed with fruit pulp is a cool and refreshing dessert for hot climates. Other fruit dishes such as compotes and mousses have also combined ingredients from both worlds. Among the compotes created in the colonial period was *mazamorra*, made with cornflour. This flour was new to both cooking worlds as it was made with corn, an American ingredient, but was invented to cater for European cooking methods.

COOKING FOR A SWEET TOOTH

It was probably the introduction of cane sugar to Latin America that brought about the most revolutionary innovations. Although honey was already in use by indigenous Americans, this was no substitute for sugar and the people of the region proved to have a very sweet tooth. In Paraguay bananas were cooked with a little lime juice and a lot of sugar until they set; today they are refrigerated before being consumed. In the past, many of the sweet things were made by nuns in convents and followed a Spanish and Portuguese tradition inherited from the Moors; others were an adaptation of local fruits or root vegetables like the candies made in Puebla from sweet potatoes, cooked and ground to a paste, flavoured artificially and moulded into decorative shapes. Sugar was also used to candy (crystallize) fruits like peaches, pears and cherries. Today a universal favourite is a caramel custard called *flan*, borrowed from Spain. Sugar-packed coconut and pumpkin desserts also abound.

Milk puddings may be the best example of the lavish use of sugar. Although they vary from place to place, they all contain rich milk cooked with sugar until thick, or even to caramel, as in the famous *cajeta* milk candy from Celaya in

Guanajuato. With the introduction of rice came rice pudding, and with bread, *capirotada* or bread pudding, a favourite during Lent when fasting forbade more meat dishes.

EL FEEVE O'CLOCK

Latin America also boasts a great array of cakes and biscuits, some plain, some elaborate. Regional specialities are cooked for weddings, christenings, engagement parties, and children's parties. Though afternoon tea in the English sense is not a Latin American tradition, some parts of Latin America have adopted what they call 'el feeve o'clock'. Chile has Elevenses, an odd name for tea at 5pm, and Argentina has its Whiskerías where sweet *empanadas* (turnovers) are notable. Of course, Latin Americans tend to be coffee drinkers and are not renowned for their tea-drinking. But if their habits were ever to change, there are plenty of cakes waiting in the wings.

Chilean Desserts

Those Chilean desserts
crumbling, white,
lovely in their meringue
drunken in their grains of sugar;
those light, dusted crystals
are deliberately made
- just as the musical recorder was made -
to summon images of the past:
lunches in shady bowers,
the red dust of summer
beneath poplar trees,
the silhouette of a lady wounded
forever at the height of a party.

... As, licking our fingers, we eat
their gentle sweetness
free from chemical, trick, or malice,
we are tasting a heaven full of angels
the pets of our childhood
a house with long corridors
where the moon sleeps
a wicker chair
and a shadow

RAÚL RIVERA

DESSERTS

Gelatina de Naranja
Orange Jelly
BOLIVIA

30g/2tablespoons unflavoured gelatine
50ml/2 fl oz water
700ml/24 fl oz orange juice
15ml/1 tablespoon lime or lemon juice
225g/8oz caster sugar
3 large eggs, well beaten

Pour the water into a small bowl and sprinkle the gelatine over it. Leave to soften. In a saucepan combine the orange and lime or lemon juice and the sugar. Stir over a low heat until the sugar has dissolved. Remove from the heat and cool. Stir in the gelatine and the water in which it has softened. Return the mixture to low heat and stir until the gelatine has dissolved. Whisk in the eggs and stir until the mixture has thickened slightly as the eggs cook. Do not let it boil. Pour into an attractive serving dish and refrigerate overnight or until set. *Serves 6.*

Dulce de Banana
Banana Mousse
PARAGUAY

5 large ripe bananas peeled and chopped
125ml/4 fl oz lime or lemon juice
175g/6oz soft brown sugar

Combine all the ingredients in a food processor and reduce to a purée. Transfer to a heavy saucepan and cook over low heat, stirring with a wooden spoon, until the purée has thickened and has the consistency of double cream. Rinse out a mould in cold water and add the purée. Refrigerate overnight. Unmould onto a serving plate by running a wet unserrated knife between the pudding and the mould, or by dipping the mould very quickly in hot water. Cover with the serving plate and invert. Serve with plain cake or by itself. *Serves 6.*

Mousse de Chocolate e Castanhas-do-Pará
Chocolate and Brazil Nut Mousse
BRAZIL

75g/3oz unsweetened (bitter) chocolate
50g/2oz caster sugar
4 large egg yolks
100g/4oz Brazil nuts, finely ground
225ml/8fl oz double cream
4 large egg whites

Break the chocolate into bits and put into the top of a double boiler set over warm water. Pour in 3 tablespoons water, stir to mix and cook over moderate heat, stirring from time to time until the mixture is smooth. Add the sugar and continue to cook until the sugar has dissolved into the chocolate. Off the heat, beat in the egg yolks one by one. Stir in the ground Brazil nuts.

Beat the cream until it stands in firm peaks and fold into the chocolate mixture. Beat the egg whites until they stand in firm peaks and fold into the mixture gently but thoroughly. Pour into a litre/1 1/4pint bowl or decorative serving dish and refrigerate overnight or for several hours. If liked, serve with sweetened whipped cream. *Serves 6.*

The wedding Blanca had not wanted was held in the cathedral, with the blessings of the bishop and a train fit for a queen, sewn by the best tailor in the country, who had performed nothing short of a miracle by disguising the prominent stomach of the bride with layers of flowers and Greco-Roman pleats. The wedding culminated in a spectacular party, with five hundred guests in evening dress who invaded the big house on the corner, enlivened by an orchestra of hired musicians, with a scandalous number of whole steers grilled with herbs, fresh seafood, Baltic caviar, Norwegian salmon, birds stuffed with truffles, a torrent of exotic liquors, a flood of champagne, and an extravagance of desserts: ladyfingers, millefeuilles, éclairs, sugar cookies, huge glass goblets of glazed fruits, Argentine strawberries, Brazilian coconuts, Chilean papayas, Cuban pineapple, and other delicacies impossible to remember, all arrayed on a long table that ran the length of the garden, terminating in a colossal three-story wedding cake designed by an Italian artist born in Naples. This man, a friend of Jean de Satigny, had transformed his humble raw materials - flour, eggs, and sugar - into a replica of the Acropolis crowned with a cloud of meringue on which rested two mythological lovers, Venus and Adonis, fashioned out of almond paste colored to imitate the rosy tones of their flesh, their blond hair, and the cobalt blue of their eyes; with them was a pudgy Cupid, also edible, which was sliced in half with a silver knife by the proud groom and the dejected bride.

ISABEL ALLENDE, **House of the Spirits**

Cachapas de Jojoto
Corn Pancakes
VENEZUELA

> 350g/12oz corn kernels, if frozen, thawed
> 175ml/6 fl oz single cream
> 1 large egg
> 4 tablespoons plain flour
> 1 teaspoon sugar
> 1/2 teaspoon unsalted butter, melted
> Butter for frying

Combine all the ingredients, except the butter for frying, in a food processor and mix to a smooth purée. Grease a non-stick frying pan by melting about 1/4 teaspoon of butter and pour in 2 tablespoons of the corn mixture. Sauté until lightly browned on both sides, a matter only of minutes. Stack and keep warm. Serve the pancakes with syrup or cheese, or jam. *Makes about 16.*

Capirotada
Bread Pudding
MEXICO

225g/8oz soft dark brown sugar
1 litre/1 1/4 pints water
5cm/2inch piece stick cinnamon
75g/3oz unsalted butter for frying and greasing
6 slices white bread, toasted and cut into 1.2cm/1/2 inch cubes
3 cooking apples, peeled, cored and chopped coarsely
100g/4oz seedless raisins
100g/4oz pine nuts, coarsely chopped
100g/4oz cheddar cheese, shredded

In a heavy saucepan combine the sugar, water and cinnamon and bring to the boil. Reduce the heat to a simmer and cook to a light syrup, about 5 minutes. Remove and discard the cinnamon and set the syrup aside.

Generously butter an ovenproof casserole. Make a layer of toast cubes, then a layer of apple, raisins, pinenuts and cheese, repeat until the ingredients are all used up. Pour the reserved syrup over and bake in a 180°C/350°Gas 4 oven for 30 minutes. Serve warm with cream, if liked. *Serves 6.*

Dulce de Leche
Milk Pudding
ARGENTINA

This may have different regional names and slight variations in ingredients and cooking methods, but basically the same pudding is eaten across Latin America. It is particularly popular in Argentina and neighbouring Chile and Uruguay.

2.5litres/4 1/2 pints rich whole milk
450g/1lb granulated sugar
1 piece vanilla bean or 1/2 teaspoon vanilla essence

In a large heavy saucepan combine the milk, sugar and vanilla and bring to a gentle simmer. Stir from time to time with a wooden spoon. As the mixture thickens, stir constantly. As soon as the bottom of the saucepan can be seen when the spoon is drawn across it, the pudding is ready for testing. Put a teaspoon of the mixture on a saucer. If it holds its shape and does not run, it is ready. Remove the vanilla bean and rinse it for another use. Put the pudding into a serving dish and serve at room temperature or slightly chilled. Serve by itself or with plain cake or ice-cream. *Serves 6.*

Budín de Zapallo
Pumpkin Pudding
ECUADOR

700g/1 1/2lb pumpkin, preferably West Indian type
1/2 teaspoon ground cinnamon
225g/8oz soft light brown sugar
125ml/4fl oz double cream
2 teaspoons unsalted butter
3 tablespoons rum
3 large eggs, well beaten

Peel and cube the pumpkin and put into a saucepan with water to cover. Bring to a boil, reduce to a simmer, cover and cook until the pumpkin is tender, about 15 minutes. Drain and add the cinnamon, sugar, cream, 1 tablespoon of the butter and the rum. Mash the pumpkin and cook it over a low heat until the sugar has melted and the mixture is well blended and fairly firm. Cool and beat in the eggs. Turn into an 8-cup soufflé dish greased with the remaining tablespoon of butter. Bake in a preheated 180°C/350°Gas 4 oven for 1 hour or until firm to the touch. Serve warm from the soufflé dish with whipped or sour cream. *Serves 6*

Away, here I am,
in search of a country,
trying hard to find myself
a land of fruit trees
to return to,
a sweet mango, perhaps,
with my mother's face
on its slowly yellowing skin,
my father's own exile
scattered among the leaves,
my brother's immaturity
and my own
nervously leaping
up and down
on the stones and trash
which hide the roots
from all of us.

ANDREW SALKEY, **Sweet Mango,** in **Facing the Sea: a Caribbean Anthology**

Flan de Piña
Pineapple Custard
COLOMBIA

This is a very old colonial recipe. In the past, pineapple juice had to be made at home, grating the fruit and making a syrup. Now that the juice is readily available in cans or cartons, it is much easier.

    50g/2oz sugar for caramelizing mould
    225g/8oz granulated sugar
    225ml/8fl oz unsweetened pineapple juice
    4 large eggs, well beaten

Put the 50g/2oz sugar into a small, heavy saucepan and set it over a low heat, stirring with a wooden spoon from time to time until the sugar melts and turns a rich caramel colour. Have ready a 6-cup soufflé dish and pour in the caramel turning the dish so that the caramel coats the bottom and the sides about half-way up. Turn the dish upside down and set aside.

In a heavy saucepan combine the sugar and pineapple juice and simmer over low heat stirring until the liquid is reduced and thickened. Cool the syrup, then pour it into the beaten eggs, beating constantly. Pour the mixture into the caramelized mould. Set the flan in a baking tin with water to come about one-third of the way up and bake in a preheated 180°C/350°Gas 4 oven. Bake until a knife inserted in the centre comes out clean, about 1 hour. Leave it to cool. To unmould, run a wet knife between the custard and the container and turn out onto a serving dish. *Serves 6.*

Mazamorra de Frutas
Fruit Compote
PERU

In Peru this would be made using purple corn (*maíz morado*), giving it a subtle, flowery, lemony taste and a beautiful, deep purple colour. Sadly this is not readily available in Europe or North America but blackberries can act as a substitute colouring agent. Honey can be used instead of sugar.

1.5l/2¹/2 pints water
450g/1lb granulated sugar
4 whole cloves
5cm/2in cinnamon stick
225g/8oz pineapple chunks, preferably fresh
450g/1lb pitted sweet cherries
2 pears, peeled, cored and sliced
225g/8oz blackberries
2 peaches, peeled, cored and sliced
225g/8oz dried apricots, halved
225g/8oz dried peaches, quartered
4 tablespoons cornflour
6 tablespoons lime or lemon juice

Combine all the ingredients except the cornflour and lime or lemon juice in a heavy saucepan. Bring to a simmer, cover and cook over a low heat for 15 minutes, or until the fruit is tender. Remove and discard the cloves and cinnamon. Mix the cornflour with a little water and stir it into the fruit mixture and cook until the liquid is thickened, a matter of minutes. Stir in the lime or lemon juice. Cool and refrigerate to chill. *Serves 8.*

Tembleque
Coconut Custard
PUERTO RICO

Tembleque means shaky, which aptly describes this custard when unmoulded. The word derives from *temblor*, meaning earthquake, a common occurrence in many parts of Latin America.

25g/1oz cornflour
125g/4oz granulated sugar
750ml/1¹/4 pints coconut milk, unsweetened, fresh or canned
2.5ml/¹/2 teaspoon almond or vanilla essence
2 large eggs, lightly beaten

In a bowl combine the cornflour and sugar and whisk in the coconut milk and almond or vanilla essence. Transfer to the top of a double boiler and cook, stirring over low heat until the mixture thickens. Whisk in the eggs and continue cooking, still stirring for 4-5 minutes longer, or until the mixture has thickened further.

Remove from the heat and leave to cool. Turn into a serving dish and refrigerate overnight so that the mixture sets properly. Unmould or serve direct from the dish. *Serves 6.*

We went out with Ma to pick fruit, she armed with a cutlass with which she hacked away thick vines and annihilated whole bushes in one swing. We returned with our baskets full of oranges, mangoes, chennettes. Ma bent under a bunch of plantains that was more than half her size.

Ma had a spot in the market on Sunday mornings, and she spent a great part of the week stewing cashews, pommes-cythères, cerises, making guava-cheese and guava jelly, sugar-cake, nut-cake, bennay-balls, toolum, shaddock-peel candy, chilibibi... On these days we hung slyly around the kitchen, if only to feed ourselves on the smells; we were never afforded the opportunity of gorging ourselves - we partook of these delicacies when Ma saw fit, and not when we desired. She was full of maxims for our edification, of which the most baffling and maddening was:

> *Who* ask
> don't get
> Who don't ask
> don't want
> Who don't want
> don't get
> Who don't get
> *don't care.*

For her one of the cardinal sins of childhood was gluttony: 'Stuff yu guts today an' eat the stones of the wilderness tomorrow.' (Ma's sayings often began on a note of familiarity only to rise into an impressive incomprehensibility, or vice versa, as in 'Them that walketh in the paths of corruption will live to ketch dey arse'.)

MERLE HODGE, **Crick Crack Monkey**

Plátanos en Gloria
Glorious Plantains
GUATEMALA

These are sometimes called, less exuberantly, *Plátanos en Jarabe* (Plantains in Syrup). Plantains - the big brothers of bananas - are eaten in many forms throughout the region, often with meat. They must be cooked before they can be eaten and may be green (unripe), half-ripe, and very ripe when the skins will be black. They are used in all three forms. In Guatemala and throughout the rest of Central America, they feature in a number of desserts.

225g/8oz light brown sugar
450ml/16fl oz water
5cm/2inch cinnamon stick
1 whole clove
3 ripe plantains, peeled and cut into 1.2cm/1/2 in diagonal slices
Corn oil for frying

In a heavy saucepan combine the sugar, water, cinnamon and clove. Simmer over a moderate heat for five minutes to make a light syrup. Remove and discard the spices and set the syrup aside. Heat enough oil in a frying pan to reach a depth of about 2.5cm/1in. Sauté the plantain slices over a moderate heat until lightly browned on both sides. Lift out and drain on kitchen towels. Add the plantain slices to the syrup and simmer over a low heat for 10-15 minutes. Serve warm. *Serves 6.*

Boniatillo
Sweet Potato Dessert
CUBA
Boniato, the white fleshed sweet potato, is the preferred type in the region. It is not as sweet as other types and is thought to have a better flavour.

450g/1lb boniatos (sweet potatoes)
350g/12 oz soft light brown sugar
125ml/4fl oz water
7.5cm/2inch cinnamon stick
10cm/4inch strip lime or lemon peel
3 eggs, well beaten
3 tablespoons rum

Peel the potatoes and slice them. Put them into a saucepan with water to cover, bring to a simmer, cover and cook until soft, about 25 minutes. Drain and reduce to a purée in a food processor.

In a heavy saucepan combine the sugar, water, cinnamon and lime or lemon peel and simmer, stirring from time to time, until it reaches 119°C/236°F on a candy thermometer. Remove and discard the cinnamon and peel. Beat in the sweet potato purée and cook over low heat, stirring constantly, until the mixture forms a heavy paste. Beat in the eggs, still over low heat and cook, still stirring for 3-4 minutes longer. Remove from the heat and stir in the rum. Cool and chill. Serve with plain cake as a dessert, or with cream. *Serves 4-6.*

When I went down to the Alene, which was due to leave the next morning, I found a swarm of men and women unloading about fifty wagons that a railway engine had left at the dockside next to the steamship. Can you guess what they contained? Bananas! I have never seen so many of them. Thousands, millions of bunches were piling up in the holds of the three ships they were loading simultaneously. The banana industry is enjoying such a boom in Panama that several steamship companies have been set up exclusively to transport them. Later on, in New York, I understood this extraordinary consumption. The streets of that city are plagued with fruit sellers, and it is common to see Yankees buy a couple of bananas as they pass by, peel them directly with their teeth, then swallow them whole without so much as slowing down. Things have reached such a state that there is a police bye-law which establishes a heavy fine for anyone who throws a banana peel in the street, thereby creating the risk that some poor unfortunate may crack his skull.

MIGUEL CANÉ, **Notas de Viaje sobre Venezuela y Colombia**

DRINKS

DRINKS

Latin America is generously endowed with drinks, both alcoholic and non-alcoholic. When the *conquistadores* arrived, they encountered a great unknown: chocolate. There were also corn-based drinks and a beer-like drink made from the sap of the century plant (*agave*), but no spirits, as distilling had not been discovered by Aztec, Maya, Inca or other Indian civilisations. The art of distilling was an Arab contribution that came via the Spanish. In due course, distilling gave the region, and the world, *tequila* made from the root stock of *Agave azul tequilana*, the blue agave. Later, when vines were established in Peru, there was *pisco*, a local brandy. When sugar-cane was introduced on the great estates of Brazil and the Caribbean islands, there was rum. Wine and beer came in due course, much of it introduced by German settlers. There are also soft drinks such as rosella or sorrel from an imported African hibiscus, *Hibiscus sabdariffa* and a drink made by steeping ripe tamarinds; orange and lemon or lime drinks made from introduced citrus fruits, and juices made from local fruits, like *guanabana* (soursop), pineapple, papaya, and coconut. The continent produces excellent coffee, particularly in Colombia and Brazil. *Mate* in Paraguay is made with the dried leaves of *Ilex paraguayensis*, non-alcoholic but mildly stimulating. Tea is not a popular drink but many tisanes, herb teas are prepared, especially camomile.

In the Aztec empire, chocolate was not merely a drink; the cacao beans were also used as currency. It was a royal drink enjoyed by the Emperor, the merchant nobility, the upper ranks of the military and the priesthood. Chocolate was forbidden to all women and many men and it was important in trade, and the great trading canoes of the Maya transported it along the coastal waters of Central America. There is some controversy over the origin of the name, which may come from two Nahuatl (language of the Aztecs) words: *xoco*, meaning bitter, and *atl*, meaning water. At that time, it had a bitter taste, though it was sometimes sweetened with honey and flavoured with vanilla. It was not necessarily taken hot but one thing in chocolate-making was constant: it was always beaten until it was foamy, sometimes by pouring it from one utensil to another, sometimes by beating. This foam was highly esteemed and people in what was once Aztec and Maya territory still like their chocolate foamy, using a Spanish *molinillo*, a carved beater, to achieve the result. After the conquest, chocolate became a favourite drink, so much so that the Church had to forbid the congregation, a great many of them women, taking cups of hot chocolate, sweetened with sugar, into mass on Sunday. Later on, milk was added to the drink and it became popular in Europe, though less so in England. Like tea and coffee, it contains caffeine so that it is mildly stimulating.

The two great fermented drinks of the Americas are *pulque*, made from the sap of agave, and *chicha*, made from corn. Pulque originates from the Aztec and Maya Empires of North and Central America, and chicha from the Inca empire of the South. Though made slightly differently in modern times, they have retained their popularity. To make pulque, the sap called *aguamiel* (honey water) from the heart of the agave plant (sometimes also called *maguey*) is collected into *acocotes*, long slender gourds, and then transferred to vats where it is left to ferment for a few days. It is best drunk fresh and is sold in *pulquerías*, as we sell draught beer in pubs. It may be plain or is often 'cured', that is flavoured, with various fruits. It is slightly more alcoholic than beer, containing about six per cent alcohol. It is an acquired taste to non-Mexicans but its popularity in its native land has endured through the centuries.

In the Inca empire, chicha, corn beer, was sacred and was made by the virgin priestesses of the Sun. It is quite alcoholic, about the same strength as pulque and has always been very popular. There is also a non-alcoholic version. Because of its sacred nature, a few drops are sprinkled on the ground before drinking in honour of Mama Sara, the Corn Goddess. There is a version made with purple corn, *chicha morada*, which has a delicate fruity taste. Fruits such as cherries and pineapple are sometimes added to this version. Chilean chicha is different altogether, as it is made from fermented grape juice, too young to be wine.

The Spanish made a distilled spirit from the *Agave azul tequilana* - tequila. The agaves are often mistakenly called cactus, though they belong to an altogether different botanical family. The spiky plant is cultivated in long rows in the state of Jalisco in Mexico and is named after the small town of Tequila. It takes twelve years for a tequila plant to reach maturity. Once the plants are harvested, the huge base, the *cabeza*, is cut out to obtain the sugary juice. White tequila is used to make mixed drinks like the *Margarita*, other tequilas, the *añejos* (aged tequilas) are smooth, to be drunk neat like a good whisky. Another tequila, called *mezcal*, from Oaxaca is often sold with a maguey grub in the bottle, though the best mezcal from Oaxaca City dispenses with this. Mexicans make a drink called *sangrita* containing tomatoes and hot chillies to accompany tequila.

With the introduction of sugar came rum of many kinds. A famous Cuban drink is *Cuba Libre* or 'Free Cuba'. It is very simple, consisting of a highball glass filled with rum, cola, lime juice and ice cubes. The significance of the drink's meaning has varied from time to time but its popularity has remained constant. An even more famous Cuban drink is the *Daiquiri*, invented in 1896 by an American engineer, Jennings Cox, who was in charge of the island's copper mines. He named it after the small town of Daiquiri in eastern Cuba, near where the mines were located. Another island rum drink that has spread around the globe is *Piña Colada*, which means strained pineapple. The drink combines coconut milk, pineapple, rum and ice cubes and whatever the maker likes to add, sometimes almond essence or vanilla, fresh mint leaves for garnish or pineapple spears. One thing is almost certain: a great many people mispronounce it as peena colada instead of peenya colada. Brazilian rum, *cachaça*, is used to make a number of drinks including *caipirinha*, one of the best known. The name translates as country bumpkin perhaps because the lime used in it is coarsely chopped, not elegantly squeezed.

'**M**escal,' said the Consul...
Sucking a lemon he took stock of his surroundings. The
mescal, while it assuaged, slowed his mind; each object demanded
some moments to impinge upon him. In one corner of the room sat a white rabbit
eating an ear of Indian corn. It nibbled at the purple and black stops with an air of
detachment, as though playing a musical instrument. Behind the bar hung, by a clamped
swivel, a beautiful Oaxaqueña gourd of *mescal de olla*, from which his drink had been
measured. Ranged on either side stood bottles of Tenampa, Berreteaga, Tequila Añejo,
Anís doble de Mallorca, a violet decanter of Henry Mallet's '*delicioso licor*', a flask of
peppermint cordial, a tall voluted bottle of Anís del Mono, on the label of which a devil
brandished a pitchfork. On the wide counter before him were saucers of toothpicks,
chillies, lemons, a tumblerful of straws, crossed long spoons in a glass tankard. At one
end large bulbous jars of many-coloured aguardiente were set, raw alcohol with
different flavours, in which citrus fruit rinds floated. An advertisement tacked by the
mirror for last night's ball in Quauhnahuac caught his eye: *Hotel Bella Vista Gran Baile a
Beneficio de la Cruz Roja. Los Mejores Artistas de la radio en acción. No falte Vd.* A scorpion
clung to the advertisement. The Consul noted all these things carefully. Drawing long
sighs of icy relief, he even counted the toothpicks. He was safe here; this was the place
he loved - sanctuary, the paradise of his despair.

The 'barman' - the son of the Elephant - known as A Few Fleas, a small dark sickly-
looking child, was glancing near-sightedly through horn-rimmed spectacles at a cartoon
serial *El Hijo del Diablo* in a boy's magazine. *Ti-to*. As he read, muttering to himself, he
ate chocolates. Returning another replenished glass of mescal to the Consul he
slopped some on the bar. He went on reading without wiping it up, however,
muttering, cramming himself with chocolate skulls bought for the Day of the Dead,
chocolate skeletons, chocolate, yes, funeral wagons. The Consul pointed out the
scorpion on the wall and the boy brushed it off with a vexed gesture: it was dead.

MALCOLM LOWRY, **Under the Volcano**

DRINKS

Chocolate

Mexican drinking chocolate is sold sweetened and flavoured with cinnamon, cloves and ground almonds.

> 450ml/16 fl oz water
> 75g/3 oz Mexican chocolate

Heat the water in a saucepan and add the chocolate, broken into bits. Simmer over moderate heat, stirring, until the chocolate dissolves. Simmer over low heat for 3-4 minutes then, off the heat, beat with a *molinillo* (little mill) or a whisk until the chocolate is frothy. If liked make the drink with milk, or a mixture of milk and water. *Serves 2.*

Atole de Leche
Milk Atole
MEXICO, GUATEMALA AND OTHER CENTRAL AMERICAN COUNTRIES

This is an ancient pre-Columbian drink which in the past was made with water, and is now more usually made with milk and water mixed.

> 65g/2$\frac{1}{2}$ oz masa harina (tortilla flour)
> 700ml/24 fl oz water
> 225g/8 oz caster sugar
> 700ml/24 fl oz whole milk
> Ground cinnamon

In a saucepan combine the masa harina and the water, cook over low heat, stirring, until the mixture has thickened. Off the heat, stir in the sugar, mixing well. Whisk in the milk, return the mixture to the heat and simmer, over low heat for 3-4 minutes. Sprinkle with a little cinnamon. Serve hot in cups or pottery mugs. *Makes 6-8 servings.*

The two Aztecs tasted the different foods and when the Spaniards saw them eating they too began to eat turkey, stew and maize cakes and enjoy the food, with much laughing and sporting. But when the time came to drink the chocolate that had been brought them, that most highly prized drink of the Indian, they were filled with fear. When the Indians saw that they dared not drink, they tasted from all the gourds and the Spaniards then quenched their thirst with chocolate and realized what a refreshing drink it was.

DIEGO DURÁN, in Sophie D. Coe, **America's First Cuisines**

Coffee

Though coffee is not indigenous to the region, Latin America rejoices in excellent coffee, sometimes served sweet and black, sometimes strong with equal amounts of milk. Mexican *Café de Olla* (Pot Coffee) is a wonderful way of serving after dinner coffee.

450ml/16 fl oz water
100g/4 oz dark brown sugar, or to taste
5cm/2inch piece stick cinnamon
2 cloves
4 tablespoons dark roast medium grind coffee
An earthenware pot

Combine the water, sugar, cinnamon and cloves in the pot and bring to a boil over moderate heat. Add the coffee, bring to the boil, stir and remove from the heat. Immediately return to the heat and bring to the boil again. Strain and serve in small pottery mugs or any demitasse cups. *Serves 2.*

Agua de Jamaica
Sorrel Drink
CARIBBEAN ISLANDS AND MEXICO

50g/2 oz sorrel (Rosella) sepals
2 litres/3 1/2 pints water
450g/1 lb granulated sugar, or to taste
2 teaspoons ground cinnamon (optional)
1/4 teaspoon ground cloves (optional)

Rinse the sorrel sepals and put them into a large saucepan with the water, sugar and spices, if using. Bring to the boil over moderate heat. Remove from the heat and infuse for 2-3 hours. Strain, pressing down on the sorrel to extract all the flavour. Refrigerate then serve in tumblers over ice cubes. If liked, 40ml/1 1/2 fl oz rum may be added to each serving. Makes about 2 litres/3 1/2 pints.

Caipirinha
Rum Sour
BRAZIL

1/2 lime, coarsely chopped, unpeeled
5ml/1 teaspoon caster sugar
50ml/2 fl oz Cachaça (Brazilian rum)
3 or 4 ice cubes

Put the lime pieces and sugar into a cocktail shaker and muddle until the sugar is dissolved in the juice from the lime and the oil from the peel. Add the rum and ice cubes and shake vigorously. Pour, unstrained, into a chilled cocktail glass. *Serves 1.*

he honey or juice of the agave is of a very agreeable sour taste. It ferments easily
on account of the sugar and mucilage which it contains. To accelerate this
fermentation they add a little old and acid pulque. The operation is terminated in three
or four days. The vinous beverage, which resembles cider, has an extremely
disagreeable odor of putrid meat, but the Europeans who have been able to get over
the aversion which this fetid odor inspires prefer pulque to every other liquor. They
consider it as stomachic, strengthening and very nutritive; it is recommended to lean
persons. I have seen whites who, like the Mexican Indians, totally abstained from water,
beer and wine and drunk no other liquor than the juice of the agave. The connoisseurs
speak with enthusiasm of the pulque prepared in the village of Cocotitlán situated to
the north of Toluca. They affirm that the excellent quality of this pulque does not
altogether depend on the art with which the liquor is prepared, but also on a taste of
the soil communicated to the juice. There are plantations of maguey near Cocotitlán
which annually bring in more than 40,000 livres (£16,661). The inhabitants of the
country differ very much in their opinions as to the true cause of the fetid odor of the
pulque. It is generally affirmed that this odor, which is analogous to that of animal
matter, is to be ascribed to the skins in which the first juice of the agave is poured. But
several well-informed individuals pretend that pulque prepared in vessels has the same
odor, and that if it is not found in that of Toluca, it is because the great cold there
modifies the process of fermentation. I only knew of this opinion at the period of my
departure from Mexico, so that I have to regret that I could not clear up by direct
experiments this curious point in vegetable chemistry. Perhaps this odor proceeds
from the decomposition of a vegeto-animal matter contained in the juice of the agave.

ALEXANDRE VON HUMBOLDT, **Political Essay on the Kingdom of New Spain**

Mate
PARAGUAY, URUGUAY, ARGENTINA

15ml/1 tablespoon mate tea
Boiling water

Rinse out a small teapot in boiling water. Add the mate tea. Pour in enough water
to make a cup of tea, stir once and let the tea steep for 5 minutes. Strain and
serve. This is usually taken plain but, if liked, add milk and/or sugar.

Frozen Daiquiri
CUBA

50ml/2 fl oz light rum
30ml/2 tablespoons lime juice
1 teaspoon caster sugar
6 ice cubes crushed

Combine the ingredients in a cocktail shaker and shake vigorously. Pour, unstrained, into a 175g/6 oz saucer champagne glass and serve with short drinking straws. *Serves 1.*

Piña Colada
PUERTO RICO

75ml/3 fl oz pineapple juice
25g/1 oz coconut cream
50ml/2 fl oz light rum
25ml/1fl oz lime or lemon juice
1/2 teaspoon almond essence or vanilla (optional)
3 or 4 ice cubes

Combine all the ingredients in a food processor and blend until smooth. If preferred use crushed ice instead of ice cubes. Pour into an 8-ounce highball glass.

One of the reasons that the Aztecs were so interested in chocolate was that their native drink *octli* (known to the Spaniards as *pulque*, a word apparently of South American origin) was mildly alcoholic, and drunkenness was not looked upon favourably by Aztec society. Octli was made of the juice of a few species of *agave*. The usual penalty for drunkenness was death. There is a considerable temperance literature among the Aztecs; and the ruler, on his accession, often gave long harangues about the sins of drink. There were countless morality tales, such as the one about the corps commander who, to pay for his drinking habit, sold off his house piece by piece, and even his weaving women, ending up lying destitute and besotted in the road. Another story told of how Nezahualcoyotl, the poet-king of Texcoco, while fleeing invaders who had butchered his father, encountered a woman during his wanderings in exile; infuriated to discover that she was cultivating agave so that she could sell octli to all comers, he slew her.

Chocolate, then, became a highly successful and culturally acceptable replacement for otli among the upper echelons of Aztec society - but even then not all would accept it. The same kind of ambivalence operated here, too, since cacao was seen as a somewhat exotic, luxurious product, foreign to the austere life to whcih they so often looked back nostalgically. Perhaps they even associated chocolate with the luxury-loving people of the hot lands, that is, the Gulf Coast and the Maya lowlands from where it originated.

SOPHIE D. COE & MICHAEL D. COE, **The True History of Chocolate**

Pisco Sour
PERU

> 10 ml/2 teaspoons egg white
> 5g/1 teaspoon caster sugar
> 10 ml/2 teaspoons lime juice
> 50 ml/2 fl oz pisco (Peruvian brandy)
> 3 or 4 ice cubes
> Angostura bitters

In a small bowl combine the egg white and sugar and stir until the sugar dissolves. Transfer to a cocktail shaker with all the other ingredients except the bitters. Shake vigorously. Strain into a small tumbler and shake a few drops of bitters on top.

Yungeño
Pisco and Orange Juice Cocktail
BOLIVIA

> 50ml/2 fl oz pisco
> 50ml/2 fl oz orange juice
> 3 or 4 ice cubes
> A chilled cocktail glass

Combine the ingredients in a cocktail shaker and shake vigorously. Pour into a cocktail glass. If liked, add the ice cubes. *Serves 1.*

Margarita
MEXICO

> 1/2 lime
> Salt
> 50ml/2 fl oz white tequila
> 1 tablespoon Triple Sec or Cointreau
> 1 tablespoon lime juice
> 3 or 4 ice cubes

Rub the rim of a cocktail glass with the cut lime and spin it in salt. In a bar glass combine the remaining ingredients and stir well to mix and chill. Strain into the prepared glass. *Serves 1.*

In the absence of tobacco, we were about to be welcomed in the village with what sixteenth-century tavellers called a *cahouin* - the Tupi-Kawahib call it *kaui* - that is, a *chicha*-drinking session. *Chicha* is made with maize, several varieties of which were grown by the natives on fire-cleared patches around the village. The early writers described the pots - as tall men - in which the liquid was prepared, and the function of the virgins of the tribe, which was to spit copious quantities of saliva into them in order to induce fermentation. Either the pots of the Tupi-Kawahib were too small or there was a shortage of virgins in the village. The three little girls were brought along and made to spit into the decoction of pounded corn. As the delicious drink, at once nutritious and refreshing, was consumed that very evening, the process of fermentation was not very far advanced.

CLAUDE LÉVI-STRAUSS, **Tristes Tropiques**

Acknowledgement of Copyrights and Sources

Frontispiece Untitled poem by Rosario Castellanos, from *Poesía No Eres Tu*,
Fondo de Cultura Económica, Mexico, 1972.

p. 8 *Popol Vuh*, quoted in Eduardo Galeano, *Memory of Fire*.

p. 10 *Notes on Mexico Made in the Year of 1822* by Joel Roberts Poinsett,
Praeger, New York, 1969.

p. 12 *Men of Maize* by Miguel Angel Asturias. © 1988 Verso, London.

p. 13 *I, Rigoberta Menchú: An Indian Woman in Guatemala* by Rigoberta Menchú.
©1983 Verso. Reprinted by permission of Verso.

p. 15 *Imperial Cusco* by Felipe Cossio del Pomar, Editorial Guaranía, Asunción
del Paraguay, 1952.

p. 27 *Mal de Amores* by Angeles Mastretta. ©1995 Seix Barral, Barcelona.

p. 34 'Journey to São Sarué', by Manoel Camilo Dos Santos, from *Brazilian
Popular Prints* edited by Mark Dineen. © 1995 Redstone Press, London.

p. 36 *Historia General del Perú, origen y descendencia de los Incas* by M. de Murua.
Translated by Nick Caistor. © 1962 Biblioteca Americana Vetus.

p. 39 *The Saint Who Did Not Believe in God* by João Ubaldo Ribeiro. Extract
translated by Nick Caistor. © 1981 editora Nova Fronteira, Rio de Janeiro.

p. 41 *Lost Cowboys* by Hank Wangford. © 1995 Victor Gollancz, London.
Reprinted by permission of Victor Gollancz.

p. 43 'Ode to Conger Chowder' from *Elemental Odes* by Pablo Neruda.
Translated by Margaret Sayers Peden. © 1991 Libris. Reprinted by
permission of Libris (for UK and Commonwealth) and University of
California Press (for USA).

p. 50 *The Conquest of New Spain* by Bernal Díaz del Castillo. © 1963
Penguin.

p. 52 *Let Me Speak! Testimony of Domitila, a Woman of the Bolivian Mines* by
Domitila Barrios de Chungara with Moema Viezzer. © 1978 Monthly
Review Press. Reprinted by permission of Monthly Review Press, New
York.

p. 55 *In Patagonia* by Bruce Chatwin. © 1977 Jonathan Cape. Reprinted by
permission of Random House (world English language rights excluding
USA) and Simon & Schuster, Inc (for USA).

p. 57 *Fire from the Mountain: the Making of a Sandinista* by Omar Cabezas.
© 1985 Jonathan Cape. Reprinted by permission of Random House (for
world English rights excluding USA, Canada and Israel) and Crown
Publishing Group (for USA).

p. 59 *Beyond the Mexique Bay* by Aldous Huxley. © 1988 Flamingo, London,
originally published by Chatto and Windus. By permission of Random
House UK Ltd on behalf of Mrs Laura Huxley.

p. 65 *The Creature in the Map* by Charles Nicholl. © 1995 Jonathan Cape,
London. Reproduced by permission of David Higham Associates.

p. 67 *The Journal of Christopher Columbus*. The Hakluyt Society, London, 1960.

p. 68 *The Spears of Twilight: Life and Death in the Amazon Jungle* by Philippe Descola. © 1996 Harper Collins, London. Reproduced by permission of Harper Collins (for UK, Commonwealth and Europe rights).

p. 71 *No Free Lunch: Food and Revolution in Cuba Today* by Medea Benjamin, Joseph Collins and Michael Scott. © 1984 Food First, San Francisco. Reprinted by permission of the Institute for Food and Development Policy.

p. 73 *Voyage of HMS Beagle, 1831-1836: Journal of Researches* by Charles Darwin, Dent, London, 1906.

p. 76 'Ode to an Onion' by Pablo Neruda. Reprinted by permission of University of California Press, Berkeley.

p. 82 *Salsa: Havana Heat, Bronx Beat* by Hernando Calvo Ospina. © 1995 Latin America Bureau, London.

p. 85 *Like Water for Chocolate* by Laura Esquivel. © Transworld. Reprinted by permission of Transworld (for U.K. and Commonwealth rights) and Doubleday U.S. (for other world English rights).

p. 87 *Lobo 1880-1893* quoted in *America's First Cuisines* by Sophie D. Coe, University of Texas Press, 1994 Austin, Texas. © 1964 Orion Press.

p. 94 'Chilean Desserts', Raúl Rivera, (1926) in *Antología de la Poesía Chilena Contemporania*, Editorial Universitaria, Santiago de Chile, 1971.

p. 96 *House of the Spirits* by Isabel Allende. © 1985 Jonathan Cape. Reprinted by permission of Jonathan Cape (world English language rights excluding USA and Canada) and Carmen Balcells Literary Agency, Barcelona (for USA and Canada).

p. 98 'Sweet Mango' by Andrew Salkey, in *Facing the Sea: a Caribbean Anthology*. © 1986 Heinemann. Reprinted by permission of Heinemann.

p. 101 *Crick Crack Monkey* by Merle Hodge. © 1970 André Deutsch, London. Reprinted by permission of André Deutsch.

p. 103 *Notas de Viaje sobre Venezuela y Colombia*, (1882), Biblioteca V Centenario Colcultura, Bogotá, 1992. Translation by Nick Caistor.

p. 108 *Under the Volcano* by Malcolm Lowry. © 1947 Jonathan Cape. Reprinted by permission of Random House (world English language rights excluding the USA) and Sterling Lord Literistic Inc (for USA).

p. 109 Diego Durán quoted in *America's First Cuisines* by Sophie D. Coe, University of Texas Press, 1994 Austin, Texas.

p. 111 *Political Essay on the Kingdom of New Spain* by Alexandre von Humboldt. © 1972 Oklahoma University Press, Norman.

p. 112 *The True History of Chocolate* by Sophie D. Coe and Michael D. Coe. © 1996 Thames and Hudson Ltd., London. Reprinted by permission of Thames and Hudson Ltd.

p. 114 *Tristes Tropiques* by Claude Levi-Strauss. © 1984 Peregrine Books, London.

Every effort has been made to identify and contact the appropriate copyright owners or their representatives. The publisher would welcome any further information.

INDEX

Spanish/Portuguese

Also published by the Latin America Bureau

If you enjoyed **The Flavour of Latin America**, you can get a further taste of the region with:

'In Focus' Country Guides
Reliable, readable and affordable guides to the people, politics and culture of different Latin American and Caribbean countries. Each guide in the series is illustrated throughout with colour and black and white photos, a 'key facts and figures' section, and fold-out map.

Titles in the series: Argentina; Bolivia; Brazil; Chile; Colombia; Costa Rica; Cuba; Dominican Republic; Eastern Caribbean; Ecuador; Guatemala; Jamaica; Mexico; Peru; Venezuela.

Salsa! Havana Heat, Bronx Beat by Hernando Calvo Ospina
A fascinating journey through the development of modern salsa, beginning on an African slave ship and ending amid the cut-throat, commercial music business of the 1990s.
Evocative use of song lyrics brings colour and passion to this lively profile of Latin dance music. **Includes FREE CD/Cassette!**

Other Latin America Bureau (LAB) books include:

* Introductions to Latin American and Caribbean society, economics, politics, and environmental issues.
* A series on Latin American and Caribbean women's lives and experiences
* Latin American authors in translation: from street gangs to salsa, from rubber tappers to guerrilla radio stations.

For a FREE copy of the Latin America Bureau's books catalogue, write to LAB, Dept FLV, 1 Amwell Street, London EC1R 1UL. Tel 0171 278 2829 Fax 0171 278 0165 E-mail lab@gn.apc.org